The Road to Hope

The Road to Hope

Responding to the Crisis of Addiction

Keaton Douglas
with Lindsay Schlegel

Our Sunday Visitor
Huntington, Indiana

Nihil Obstat
Msgr. Michael Heintz, Ph.D.
Censor Librorum

Imprimatur
✠ Kevin C. Rhoades
Bishop of Fort Wayne-South Bend
November 21, 2022

The *Nihil Obstat* and *Imprimatur* are official declarations that a book is free from doctrinal or moral error. It is not implied that those who have granted the *Nihil Obstat* and *Imprimatur* agree with the contents, opinions, or statements expressed.

Our Sunday Visitor Publishing Division
Our Sunday Visitor, Inc.
200 Noll Plaza
Huntington, IN 46750
www.osv.com
1-800-348-2440

ISBN: 978-1-63966-000-1 (Inventory No. T2741)
1. RELIGION—Christian Ministry—Counseling & Recovery.
2. RELIGION—Christian Ministry—General.
3. RELIGION—Christianity—Catholic.

eISBN: 978-1-63966-001-8
LCCN: 2023931908

Cover and interior design: Chelsea Alt
Cover and interior art: Adobe Stock

PRINTED IN THE UNITED STATES OF AMERICA

This book is dedicated to all those who are suffering from the disease of addiction and their families. May they find the peace only Christ can provide, as well as consolation in the Holy Roman Catholic Church.

To Mary, the Blessed Mother of God, our mother, and the mother of the universal Church, who guides all that I do. I echo the mantra of Pope St. John Paul II: "Totus tuus" — I am all yours!

To Fr. Thomas Augustine Judge, CM, ST, whose work in the "tangled portion of the Vineyard" inspires everything I do. May the Holy Spirit continue to inspire us all in our apostolic mission every day of our lives.

To Ron Reinhart, my mentor and colleague, who taught me how to see those suffering with addictions through Christ's eyes and to love them with his heart. May you rest in peace.

unbearable

the pain in your eyes,
unbearable to see.
rushing to you
my impulse to stay close,
don't let go, carry you through.

and your Christ eyes,
pierce my soul.
my God, my God,
I can't abandon you!

the reality, waiting.
no intrusiveness upon your agony.
slack with grief watching you,
breathing in and out to pass the time,
tiredness all around you.

and your Christ eyes,
pierce my soul.
my God, my God,
I can't abandon you!

resignation overtaking you
and I am silent.
waiting for the moment
to embrace you, absorb you,
pull you through me;
suffering cast out.

and your Christ eyes,
pierce my soul.
my God, my God,
I can't abandon you!

Lynn O'Gorman Latchford
"*ad deificum lumen*" Prologue RB
"The holy cross be my light"
Et Facta Est Lux

Contents

Contents

Introduction

It's Not Someone Else's Problem

We all know someone.

Someone struggling with substance use disorder, that is. Nearly one in five Americans aged twelve or older reported illicit drug use in 2018,[1] and that was before COVID-19 threw our culture into further isolation. With the numbers as they are, it's nearly impossible for anyone in the United States to *not* know someone battling an addiction to drugs or alcohol. The someone might be an immediate family member. The someone could be a neighbor, someone you went to high school with, or a friend's sibling or child. The someone may be you. One way or another, the plague of substance use disorders affects our society as a whole, and it affects each and every one of us as individuals.

So why do so many of us think that this crisis, this epidemic, which long preceded the COVID-19 pandemic, is someone else's problem?

Perhaps the stigma around substance use disorder, the way it's spoken of in whispered voices and hushed tones — even when someone loses his life — makes us feel the issue is taboo. The reason could be that many of us simply don't understand the nature of addiction as a disease of mind, body, and spirit. Or maybe we wouldn't know where to start helping those who have experienced something that looks so different from the way our own lives have played out thus far.

That attitude may be where we are, but it can't be where we stay. As a Church, we have a responsibility to tend to the least among us. We need to be the Good Samaritan rather than the priest who passes the needy person by. We are called to build relationships with and to accompany those who are far from Christ. We have a mission to bring his everlasting love and all-powerful mercy to those souls most in need of it.

These souls are in our communities, in our parishes, and they are thirsting. They are dying.

People suffering from addiction may seem "other" to us. Nearly a decade ago, I too had no clue how to relate to someone who is a slave to a chemical each and every day. But the reality is we are all prone to unruly behavior. For some of us, that spiritual malady gives way to chemical or behavioral habits that become all-encompassing. We don't know what Saint Paul suffered with, but we know he wrote to the Romans, "I am carnal, sold under sin. I do not understand my own actions. For I do not do what I want, but I do the very thing I hate. ... For I know that nothing good dwells within me, that is, in my flesh. I can will what is right, but I cannot do it. For I do not do the good I want, but the evil I do not want is what I do" (Rom 7:14–15, 18–19).

Dr. Gerald G. May — the late psychiatrist, spiritual director, and author of *Addiction & Grace: Love and Spirituality in the Heal-*

ing of Addictions — wrote, "Whether we are consciously religious or not, this desire [for God] is our deepest longing and our most precious treasure."[2] At the same time, we all have things in our lives we don't want to think about or feel — what we might picture as a mental pile of repressed memories. Some have been hurt by those they should have been able to trust, and so they cannot fathom a loving Father. Others seek a way to numb pain from early childhood trauma, be it emotional, physical, or sexual abuse or some other feeling of abandonment. In any case, when we don't develop coping skills to deal with our mental piles, our human nature searches for some means to mitigate that pain. This behavior may be learned, or it might be a reaction to having no better option. The result is that, despite the universal hunger "to love, to be loved, and to move closer to the Source of love," we turn away from love for ourselves, for others, and for God.[3]

Repression Versus Addiction

May understood the two forces that turn us away from love — again, two forces from which we all suffer in one way or another — to be *repression* and *addiction*. Repression, he wrote, is "relatively flexible," in that while we can repress our desire for love (usually to minimize the potential for suffering), the desire remains in us, so that we can return to it when we're ready to be vulnerable.[4]

Addiction, on the other hand, is "much more vicious." May wrote that addiction "abuses our freedom and makes us do things we really do not want to do" (hello again, Saint Paul!).[5] Addictions come to rule our lives in ways that repressions do not because addiction "*attaches* desire, bonds and enslaves the energy of desire to certain specific behaviors, things, or people."[6] For a long time, the word "attachment," which comes from a French word that means "nailed to," was used to describe this process. We can see how "nailing" our desire to something else — desire which is meant to be turned toward God, others, and the self — can escalate and become an addiction. We're looking for the deepest desire of who we were created to be, but we're looking for it in places where we will never find it.

Addiction as Attachment

We all suffer from attachments: things that keep us from developing true intimacy with God. The object of attachment differs from person to person. Some become attached to material goods or modern-day false idols like pride and prestige, while others become attached to behaviors and substances. The tendency to allow something to come between ourselves and the good, between ourselves and God, is the same. I use the terms "unnatural attachment" and "addiction" interchangeably, because "unnatural" points to how the attachment goes beyond the scope of things in our day-to-day lives. In May's language, addictions "enslave us with chains that are of our own making and yet that, paradoxically, are virtually beyond our control."[7] And while addiction is "the absolute enemy of human freedom, the antipathy of love," it can also "lead us to a deep appreciation of grace. [It] can bring us to our knees."[8]

Human nature hasn't changed in 2,000 years. Every single one of us has a disordered attachment to something, often as a symptom of a deeper issue with guilt, shame, abandonment, or desolation. Whatever we are attached to, our attachment is our attempt to fill the void in our lives that only the God who made us and loves us can fill. Maybe your attachment hasn't caused you to lose your job, your home, your health, or the relationships with the ones you love. But to some degree, we all need to be healed, to be made whole, to be redeemed. Appreciating the universality of brokenness is the first step to understanding addiction as a spiritual disease.

Understanding Addiction as Catholics

Too often, recovery is approached from either a purely religious or a purely secular point of view. I certainly do not mean to suggest that prayer, on its own, is the answer for healing from addiction. Human beings are complex creations, and recovery means tending to the physical, emotional, and mental elements of addiction, as well as the spiritual.

This comprehensive understanding of the human being is only one way in which the Catholic tradition is uniquely poised to tend to this societal malady. We know that human beings are body *and* soul. We profess honoring the dignity of every human life. We preach the value of redemptive suffering.

But we, as a Church, lack an education on what addiction is from physical, emotional, mental, and spiritual perspectives. We can't help remedy a problem if we don't understand it. Once we're educated, we can begin to equip ourselves to be the hands and feet of Christ for those on the journey of recovery and for the family and friends who ache for them. We can recognize that their problem is our problem, too.

God Calls into Service Those Least Likely

I am the last person in the world you would expect to pioneer an addiction recovery program.

Before God led me to Trinity House at the Shrine of St. Joseph in Stirling, New Jersey in 2014, I hadn't had a personal experience with someone who had struggled with or lost his or her life to a substance use disorder. I was a Wall Street assistant vice president-turned-professional singer who rode horses on my farmland in my spare time. Though I lived not far from Paterson, New Jersey, then the epicenter of heroin trafficking in the Northeast, this scourge on our nation hadn't yet hit home for me.

But then, God often chooses the least likely vessel for his work. Why else would he have called Saul, a Hebrew zealot and the worst persecutor of the early Christians, to his service, turning him into Paul, arguably the greatest evangelizer of the Christian faith? Why else would he have chosen Abraham and Sarah, an aged, barren couple, to be the father and mother of his people, the ones on whom he would bestow his holy covenant through the birth of their miracle child, Isaac, born to them in their later years? Why would he have his only-begotten Son, the King of kings, Jesus, born to a humble maiden and her chaste spouse in the least likely of places, a lowly manger on the outskirts of the city of Jerusalem?

I suppose God is funny that way. He calls his people from all different walks of life to serve him as he sees fit. Everyone. He calls everyone, not only the holy ones whose names we've learned through Sacred Scripture, but you and me, too.

Before December 2014, had you asked what I perceived my life's vocation to be, I might not have given you any answer at all. I was a singer earning a living as a full-time musician, which was a feat in and of itself. Though my name wasn't familiar to many, I'd had the opportunity to perform at some major events, like presidential inaugural balls. I was proud of the fact that I had chosen to leave a comfy Wall Street position to follow my heart's desire. I was a wife and a mother, and I was happy.

Things were humming along until I ran headfirst into the unexpected demise of my first marriage. On my thirty-third birthday — the start of what some would call my "Jesus year" — I learned that not only had my husband been unfaithful, but he'd set up another whole life in the next town over with another woman. When he left me that day, there wasn't anything in our home that he valued enough to take with him to his new home. He discarded everything he'd known from our life as though it were useless debris. Sitting atop the mound was me.

The following eight years were filled with anger and resentment — at my ex for not being able to live up to his vow; at God for allowing this to happen to me, who had obeyed all the rules;

at the woman who had no problem stepping into my shoes. For eight years I allowed the unforgiveness inside me to corrode me like venom — until one unexpected day, when that woman asked for my forgiveness. And to my surprise, I forgave her.

Who was this God who, by lifting the burden of unforgiveness, had made room for himself in my heart in a single minute?

I found myself drawn back to the faith of my childhood. My reversion to the Catholic Faith had begun. Through the Rosary and the sacraments, I came home to Christ and his Church, largely through the Blessed Mother. I began to speak frequently, witnessing to my call back to the Church and encouraging forgiveness and healing. Because of my professional training as an entertainer, I enjoyed sharing my reversion story and soon became the toast of many a Rosary Society and communion breakfast at churches throughout the state.

When I was invited to speak at a Catholic retreat center in December 2014 to twenty-five women in recovery, mostly from heroin addiction, the event was the only time I can remember being petrified to speak in front of an audience. What did I know about substance use disorders? Really, next to nothing.

"Why would they ever want to listen to me?" I asked Ron, the retreat director. "I'm not in recovery. I've never even smoked pot."

But Ron encouraged me, assuring me that these women didn't want to talk only to other people in recovery. "Do you think there's nothing you can teach them?" he asked me. "Do you think there's nothing *they* can teach you?"

His answer startled me. I silently upbraided myself for being so close-minded. He was right. I didn't think they could teach me anything. But that day, they taught me everything.

I remember every detail about that first talk. I entered the meeting room, stood in the center, and sang the first stanza of "Amazing Grace." I told the women that I wasn't working a Twelve Step program, because I wasn't addicted to either drugs or alcohol.

I still expected to get tossed out of the room. Instead they looked at me and listened. I unfolded my story before them. I told them of being broken and then made whole again, of forgiving in a way that cracked open a hardened heart, of rediscovering prayer and the sacraments. Like theirs, it was a story of brokenness and resentment, of love and loss.

When I started to weep, they did too. I talked to them of my long journey of faith and my new life in Christ, of welcoming the redeeming grace of the Savior into my life in so powerful a way that I now seek to serve him with all I have. My life had done a one-eighty to serve him alone. When I finished, there were tears and hugs all around. They had not judged me for not being addicted, and they realized that I had not judged them for their addictions.

The welcome I received that day, not as a person in recovery — because I wasn't — but as a child of God broken by this world and redeemed by his Blood, was the beginning of finding my life's vocation in educating addicted persons and their families about the spiritual component of addiction and the necessity of a spiritual conversion for recovery. First, though, I had to learn these things myself.

As I gave my "fiat" to continuing with the recovery ministry and becoming a regular member of the retreat team, a desperate phone call from my nephew looking for help for his friend landed a young man with beautiful, soul-wrenching blue eyes in my path. John was twenty-eight years old, sometimes snarky, sometimes sweet, and still addicted to heroin. Again, I thought I had nothing to offer him. I couldn't relate to his experience. I didn't know what to say to him. I had no idea what to do. I felt lost, humbled, and once again broken.

I railed against God, fists in the air. "What am I supposed to do with him? I work with people in recovery! They're already sober. I don't know what to do with him! Why did you give him to me?"

I didn't get an answer right away. But I trusted that John had been given to me for a reason.

All I could do for him, for his exhausted mother, for his heart-broken family, was love him. And love him I did, first by my own determination but later, when I didn't think I could handle any more, by the amazing grace of God.

Through my experience accompanying John on his long journey of struggle and brief moments of sobriety, God opened more doors before me. He sent me more invitations to love, more souls in need of grace and mercy, whom I came to call my birds. I was learning that the gifts of love, grace, and mercy are not mine to give but are given for his love. The experience with John was changing my life.

Our Mission as Catholics: Spiritual Companionship

Early on, John was my sole focus, but now, as the executive director of iTHIRST (which stands for The Healing Initiative — Recovery, Spirituality, and Twelve Steps), I have encountered hundreds more Johns. I have done my best to treat each with dignity and respect, to approach every one with the love of the Father. There are more souls in need than one person can care for. So today, my mission is to teach others to become iTHIRST spiritual companions (ITSCs).

The mission is more urgent now than ever before. Why? Because from March 2020 to April 2021, more than 100,000 people perished because of a drug overdose, a nearly thirty percent increase from the year before.[9] That's more than a stadium's worth of our brothers and sisters losing their lives on an annual basis. That number doesn't include alcohol-related deaths, nor does it include people who are still using. We, the Church, are called to serve these least brothers and sisters. As a Church, we *need* to serve these brothers and sisters. We need to not be afraid to stand in the margins, to get dirty and smell like the sheep, as Pope Francis would say.[10] We have a responsibility to minister to men, women, mothers, fathers, coworkers, aunts, uncles, and friends in recovery.

Since COVID-19 hit, money allocated for substance use and mental health disorders has been redirected. The resources earmarked for this population have vanished. Now, more than ever, the Church needs to be present as Christ's hands and feet. As the Blessed Mother Mary does for us, her children, we are called to point all these to her Son, the Savior. I think of myself as the handmaid of the Handmaid, and I invite you to do the same.

The Purpose of This Book

In these pages, you will see inside the raging epidemic of substance use disorders in our country and come to better understand it. At the start of each chapter, you will hear from someone in recovery or, in three cases, from someone else very close to this mission, including the mother of a young man lost to opioid use, a priest of the Missionary Servants of the Most Holy Trinity, and the mother of a son in recovery whose whole family has been affected by addiction. Over the course of this book, you will learn how addiction is a disease of mind, body, and spirit. And wherever you are in your life and on your journey with the Lord, this book will equip, empower, and encourage you to start making real change in your community. Because I can guarantee you there's someone — more than some*one*, but many someones — who needs it.

I can show you from my experience that God knows what he's doing, even when he calls us to situations that seem beyond our capabilities. There is no love without sacrifice. True sacrifice, sincere abandonment to God's will, always bears fruit more powerfully life-giving than anything we might have done on our own. It's messy, challenging, and often devastating work. But someone needs to do it. I need to do it. You need to do it. And for the sake of those least among us, we need to start right now.

1

We Are Not Immune

In the early days of his addiction to prescribed opiates, my son would say, "Mom, I'm gonna fix myself." I had no idea what he meant, nor that he was addicted to the pills a doctor prescribed, and kept prescribing, after a minor surgery. You fix something that's broken, and as I reflect on it now, I see his emerging realization that those pills had broken him.

After fifteen years of my son's struggle to fix that brokenness, the Lord took him to himself. Those years broke me, too, as I tried to walk with him in his suffering. The sorrow of it stops me in my tracks when it comes crashing down. It makes it hard to do everything. It makes me slow. It makes those tears that are always there just waiting to be set free run like rivulets.

So now I walk this path, carrying both my own and

his wounds with me. And in a way that makes no sense in human terms, but complete sense in God's — that woundedness, mine and his together, has become my greatest treasure. The flip side of my woundedness is that heart open and yearning to pour out the healing balm of love for others who are wounded as my son was.

Finally, I see the true sacredness of the wounds of Our Lord. When he appeared to the disciples in the upper room, those wounds were still there, not magically healed, but gaping enough for Thomas to put his finger into. Our Lord's wounds remain, as do our own wounds. By the grace of these wounds, we are able to share in both his suffering and each other's.

— Melinda

E ach and every human being is created in love, by love, and for love, to be in communion with our Creator. I state this as fact, because I know it to be so through lived experience, academic Scriptural study, and the work I do every day as a consultant, educator, and counselor and as the founder and executive director of iTHIRST. The contemporary take on this age-old truth might be to say that we all desire to be seen and known. Semantics can't change how deeply this reality lies within the human person. This thirst for love is inherent in what it is to be human, to be a creation of the Creator.

Just as we are all called to love and be loved, we human beings are also universally broken in one way or another. Anecdotally, I have found that the great majority of the people with whom I work have suffered some kind of early childhood trauma or abuse. These wounds are not easily processed and can become repressed, creating the propensity to look elsewhere for consolation. Even those who did not suffer greatly in childhood carry their own wounds inflicted by any variety of situations.

Our Mutual Woundedness

Our mutual woundedness is our key to understanding any suffering. Even when wounds are inflicted by different instruments or objects, we all experience brokenness in our lives. Painful as this can be, it is also a profound gift. Through the prism of our own suffering, we can mirror the suffering of others. This is what the late Dutch priest and theologian Henri Nouwen had in mind when he wrote about the "wounded healer." He describes how those who minister to others can make the deepest connection to their God through their personal suffering — and can make their deepest connection to those who are vulnerable and marginalized through their shared suffering. Nouwen wrote:

> Nobody escapes being wounded. We are all wounded people, whether physically, emotionally, mentally, or spiritually. The main question is not "How can we hide our wounds?" so we don't have to be embarrassed, but "How can we put our woundedness in the service of others?" When our wounds cease to be a source of shame, and become a source of healing, we have become wounded healers.
>
> Jesus is God's wounded healer: through his wounds we are healed. Jesus' suffering and death brought joy and life. His humiliation brought glory; his rejection brought a community of love. As followers of Jesus we can also allow our wounds to bring healing to others.[1]

I don't have the experience of suffering from substance use disorder, but it doesn't matter what breaks us. What matters is what happens to us in the midst of our brokenness.

When I spoke to those women on retreat in December 2014, I was honest and transparent about my experience of anger at the world and at God. I spoke about feeling isolation, unworthiness, guilt and shame at not being able to hold my marriage together and about my deep embarrassment over not even knowing it was falling apart. And I shared a powerful experience of forgiveness that shook me, changed me, and invited me back into intimacy with the God of my understanding.

It was these deep-seated realities of being broken and redeemed in my faith that the women were interested in and attentive to. What had broken me was adultery. What had broken them was addiction. From that place of brokenness we found a way to understand each other, and I received an unexpected and tremendously powerful gift. Compassion. Love. Those women changed my life that day. They taught me that what we have in common as wounded children of God is far greater than we don't have in common because of the specifics of our lives.

I saw Christ in them and they saw themselves in me. We had all suffered loss. We all knew we thirsted for something else.

Our Common Thirst

What we thirsted for is communion with God. In the Book of Genesis, we read, "Then God said, 'Let us make man in our image, after our likeness'" (Gn 1:26). Nothing else in Creation shares this connection with the Creator. Nowhere in the earth, the plants, or the animals is God imaged the way he is in the human person. We understand this imaging to be the image of love. Saint John writes in his first letter, "Beloved, let us love one another; for love is of God, and he who loves is born of God and knows God. He who does not love does not know God; for God is love" (1 Jn 4:7–8). May explains that God's grace "is a gift that we are free to ignore, reject, ask for, or simply accept. And it is a gift that is often given in spite of our intentions and errors."[2] We are made for communion. We are made for relationship. We are made for giving and receiving. More particularly, we are made to be free to give and receive love.

Jesus confirms this in the Gospel of Matthew, where he reveals the two greatest commandments. "And he said to him, 'You shall love the Lord your God with all your heart, and with all your soul, and with all your mind. This is the great and first commandment. And a second is like it, You shall love your neighbor as yourself. On these two commandments depend all the law and the prophets'" (Mt 22:37–40). Our purpose in life, our reason for living, is ultimately to love and be loved by our Creator and to love and be loved by our fellows. We manifest this purpose by accepting his invitation to be in relationship with him, by claiming his love as the source of our dignity, and by loving others and recognizing the same God-given dignity in them.

When appreciated this way, love takes many forms, such as individual and communal prayer, acts of service, friendship, consecrated life, family life, single life, feeding the hungry, clothing the naked, correcting the sinner, and so on. Most would agree these are noble and worthwhile pursuits. So then why do we ever do anything to the contrary?

Just as it is true that we are all created in, by, and for love, so it is true that we are hindered by disordered attachments that interfere with giving and receiving love with God, others, and ourselves. We are all prone to unruly behaviors. Some take a seemingly more drastic toll than others, but make no mistake: We are none of us immune. We each have some propensity that enslaves us, keeping us from the freedom and love God has created us for.

iTHIRST was created with the desire to quench God's thirst for love and to make known his desire to quench our thirst for love. These words, "I thirst," have two sources. They were among the last words Jesus spoke from the cross (see Jn 19:28), and they were foundational to St. Teresa of Calcutta's call within a call to respond to those dying in the streets of her city. She wrote of her order:

> "I Thirst," Jesus said when He was deprived of every
> consolation, when He was dying in Absolute Poverty,
> when He was left alone, despised. ... He spoke of His
> Thirst — not for water but for love, for sacrifice. Jesus is
> God; therefore His love — His thirst is infinite. The Aim
> of our Society is to quench this infinite thirst of God
> Made Man. ... The Missionary of Charity must always
> be with Our Lady at the foot of the Cross ... to quench
> the burning thirst of Jesus."[3]

Missionary of Charity or not, we all must come to the foot of
the cross if we intend to authentically follow Christ. When I
teach about those two great commandments from the Gospel
of Matthew, I first reach my hands above my head, heavenward,
to denote the relationship in the first commandment, that love
of God, that intimacy with the Father. Then I stretch my arms
to my sides to denote love of brothers and sisters in the second
commandment. Those actions — arms lifted overhead and then
stretched to the sides — trace the cross itself, the sign of the
greatest love one can have: "that a man lay down his life for his
friends" (Jn 15:13). Such an act of self-gift is total. It's complete. It
does not allow room for anything else to get in the way.

But something can and does get in the way: addiction.

Choosing Something Other Than God

Addiction is really a desperate response to our desire to fill a
hole in the soul that only God can fill. May suggests that addiction reenacts the Fall of our first parents. He writes that our
spiritual ancestors opened the door for us, that the story of Eden
is "simply repeating itself endlessly through history" in episodes
of temptation, self-centeredness, pride, rebelliousness, curiosity,
and desire.[4] The Lord offers us freedom and love, yet we choose
something else, something we mistakenly believe will satisfy our

desire and will quench the thirst that only God's love is capable
of satiating.

We have chosen something else again and again throughout salvation history. Consider Noah, who got drunk after God
made the covenant with him and then "lay uncovered in his tent"
(Gn 9:21). Or recall the way drunkenness is described in Prov-
erbs: "[Wine] goes down smoothly. / At the last it bites like a
serpent, / and stings like an adder. / Your eyes will see strange
things, / and your mind utter perverse things" — yet the desire
for drink remains (see Prv 23:31–33, 35).

Whether or not we personally struggle with substance use
disorder, we all struggle with disordered attachments to something worldly. Perhaps we respond to our emotions by eating.
Maybe we succumb to the thrill of gambling. We might find ourselves unable to refuse lustful inclinations.

Or it could be that our own attachments don't seem so extreme. We scroll aimlessly through social media, but we're sure
we're not hurting anyone. We default to turning on the television
every evening, even though we're not interested in what's on. We
dodge the text message from a relationship that asks too much
of us. We keep what we might otherwise give.

In each of these situations, from the seemingly extreme to
the seemingly mundane, we choose something other than love
of God. We don't give of ourselves in a healthy way to others.
These choices — which may not even seem like choices in the
moment — come from that brokenness, that thirst, we all share.
We look inward instead of outward. We place our hope in something that can't supply what we seek, if we dare to hope at all.

In his book *Catholicism: A Journey to the Heart of the Faith*,
Bishop Robert Barron calls on the wisdom of St. Thomas Aquinas, who suggested that most attachments fall into one of four
categories: wealth, pleasure, power, or honor. "Sensing the void
within, we attempt to fill it up with some combination of these

four things, but only by emptying out the self in love can we make the space for God to fill us," Bishop Barron explains.[5] He continues:

> When we try to satisfy the hunger for God with some-thing less than God, we will naturally be frustrated, and then in our frustration, we will convince ourselves that we need more of that finite good, so we will struggle to achieve it, only to find ourselves again, necessarily, dissat-isfied. At this point, a sort of spiritual panic sets in, and we can find ourselves turning obsessively around this crea-turely good that can never in principle make us happy.[6]

When I teach about unnatural attachments, I put my hand, which stands in as the object of attachment, right in front of my face. In this stance, the only things I can see are myself and my hand. I see nothing beyond it. Addiction precludes us from seeing, much less choosing, anything other than what we're attached to.

A Definition of Addiction

In clinical terms, May defines addiction as "a *state* of compulsion, obsession, or preoccupation that enslaves a person's will and de-sire. Addiction sidetracks and eclipses the energy of our deepest, truest desire for love and goodness."[7] Furthermore, he writes that addiction "limits the freedom of human desire … caused by the attachment, or nailing, of desire to specific objects."[8]

May lays out five characteristics of true addiction:

1. **tolerance**, the phenomenon of needing or wanting ever more of the addictive substance, behavior, or object;
2. **withdrawal**, which can manifest as either a stress reaction (when the body subconsciously sends dan-ger signals, such as irritability or tremors, to show

something is wrong) or as a rebound reaction (the opposite of the symptoms of the addictive behavior, experienced when the body senses it isn't going to get what it thinks it needs);

3. **self-deception**, the many mind tricks that the afflicted person uses to rationalize his or her behavior;

4. **loss of willpower**, the battle between the desire to stop and the inability to stop, which ultimately leads to a devastating loss of self-esteem; and

5. **distortion of attention**, the inability to connect with anyone or anything other than that which he or she is attached to.[9]

Those who are addicted may also experience negative effects on physical or emotional health, take dangerous action in pursuit of the behavior, and be incapable of discussing the behavior with others.

To see this in action, let's take, for example, a gambler who goes to Atlantic City twice a year and each time loses a tremendous amount of money. At a certain point, she stops going to Atlantic City but gambles instead online. She rationalizes that her behavior is less of a problem because she's not spending money and time to drive to the casino. At the same time, she's breaking into her 401K or her kid's college fund to have more money to use. When that doesn't suffice and she's still trying to satisfy this desire, she begins making arrangements with loan sharks. Meanwhile, she's unable to talk with anyone about what's going on. This compulsion is a case of an attachment that has become so perversely disordered that it prevents her from opening herself to intimacy with God, others, and herself. It's become an addiction.

It bears repeating that we cannot undertake the journey of walking with addicted persons if we do so with an us-versus-them mentality. Perhaps no situation in your own life has gotten that clearly out of control. But let's not forget our spiritual ancestors, who wrestled with golden calves. And let's be honest that many of us wrestle with a desire to be known, to be esteemed, or to possess a degree of prestige or power in our corner of the world.

Addiction as a Spiritual Malady

The hallmarks of addiction as a disease — shame, guilt, abandonment, and desolation — are ultimately part of one's spiritual condition. But when I say that, I don't mean that some people have spirits that are somehow inferior (or superior) to others. Suffering is a common experience. This is why I could connect with those women on retreat. This common ground is why I believe that each member of the Body of Christ, each member of the Church, is called to respond to those brothers and sisters of ours who struggle with addiction and to their families.

Addiction is not something new. People have suffered since the beginning of time. But in our time, the rules have changed, especially due to the opioids in our communities and how they got there (more on that in chapter 2). And while today there are resources out there for people who are suffering from addictions and for their families, most are missing the most important element of lasting recovery: the hope not just of sobriety but of abundant life, of connection, of community.

The Role of Community

Community is an important building block of society. Community provides identity, safety, and a sense of belonging to an individual, a family, or a group. Each one of us belongs to many communities: where we work, where we live, where we socialize, and so on. This need for connection is why sponsorship is a crucial element of Twelve Step programs: Often those who suffer need to rebuild social connections and circles that exclude the addictive behaviors they seek to eschew.

Koinonia is the Greek word for togetherness in Christ, and it exemplifies what May stated about community:

> Undergirding God's mysterious love for us as individuals is the even more wondrous way grace comes to us in community. ... At intersections of paths through space that only God can chart, we are drawn together in systems of shared histories, we form covenants, and we become traditions, churches, communities of faith. Here our energies coalesce, and grace pours through the spaciousness of our communal solitude, through our intimacy and interdependence, and, with exponential brilliance, through the sacramental gatherings of true community.[10]

Community is the opposite of isolation, which is another trademark of addiction. Whereas addiction is inward-facing, life in community is about looking toward the other, about belonging in a group, about finding one's herd. This desire, when misguided, is often what leads someone down a path that leads to addiction. I've also seen that this desire, when redirected to the ultimate koinonia, that is, the Catholic Church, can offer hope of a lasting and abundant recovery. To put it bluntly, no community provides greater comfort in times of great tumult, provides more resonating consolation amidst the struggles and challenges of life, than the Church. The Church has been providing this comfort, this consolation, for two thousand years, and we need to do so in a more prominent and far-reaching mode today.

The Church and the Road to Hope

I often talk metaphorically about the Road to Hope — the journey from the abyss of addiction back to the light and love of recovery, where those who suffer can once again freely acknowledge the grace and love that God has continued to pour upon them.

For many, the idea of the Church's involvement in an individual's recovery might seem curious. What does the Church know about addiction and recovery? The answer, borne out in Sacred Scripture, is this: plenty. What so many fail to realize is that recovery can only come about when an individual ends the self-isolation that so characterizes addiction and returns to community.

Our Church is a living example of May's systems of shared histories coming to life through the common history of our beliefs in our Nicene Creed. We are people of a covenant; we worship together; we collectively allow the power of the Holy Spirit to move in our midst. We acknowledge and accept the call to serve. And in so doing, we, as the Church, have a real responsibility to those who suffer from addictions.

When I see someone suffering, I have the gift of seeing them the way God sees them. I see who they could be, who God intended them to be, even when neither they nor seemingly anyone else around them can see it. This is an approach we can all develop through prayer and training. This mindset may come more naturally to some than others (again, our piles may play a role), but we are all on this journey to Heaven together. We are called to help each other on the way.

As creations of the Creator, we are incomplete without his love. We are only complete when we welcome God into our days, into our hearts, and into the dark places in our lives. When we do, we can restore the love that has been distorted. We can again embrace the commandments that tell us who we are and what we're called to do and be. This restoration is what we call recovery.

So much pain and suffering surfaces when we work with people struggling with addictions and with substance use disorders in particular. The twist is that this pain and suffering are exactly what give us the key to reestablish communion, harmony, and life.

Reflect

- Recall times when you have felt wounded or broken. Contemplate what caused your sense of brokenness at those times. How might your own experiences with brokenness help you accompany another?
- God's love and mercy are truly ineffable, yet he gives us an opportunity either to accept his love and mercy freely or to ignore it, even to reject it. When in your life have you chosen to ignore or reject God's love and mercy and instead to walk away from him?
- Communities, starting with families, are the most important building blocks of society, where an individual can find identity and purpose and from where they can derive solutions to all sorts of issues. Why, in your opinion, might the koinonia — community in Christ — be the best community to turn to in times of great tumult, both societally and personally?

Pray

God and Father, Giver of all good things, we know you have poured out your love and mercy on us, like a fountain that washes us clean.

Grant that we never turn from that love and mercy again, but turn to it and to you in all times of turmoil and tumult, with child-like trust.

Grant that we may embrace our own brokenness and draw nearer to you because of it, just as we pray to see you in the suffering and brokenness of our brothers and sisters.

May we never seek to be self-serving or self-sufficient, for of and by ourselves we are just empty jars. Like the empty jars at Cana, we pray you fill us with the wine of your benevolence and the will of your love.

Amen.

❧

2

The Spiritual Elephant
in the Room

*I searched for a kind God in so many rooms during active
addiction. I looked for a God that would tell me he did not
create me in error. Never could I have imagined I would
have found God in the hug of a human being. The addict is
one of the loneliest spirits that walk amongst us, constantly
seeking an abyss that hides their pain.*

*I was in rehab and was told I was going to a retreat
for the weekend with several other men. We arrived in a
van somewhere in a beautiful location, very different from
the filthy streets I was used to. Standing on the porch in
the distance to greet us was this small-statured woman. As
we approached this stoic-looking home, the woman on the
porch took each one of the men in her arms and hugged*

them. When it was my turn, she looked at me and smiled.
She could see I was not used to being touched, but what was
destined to happen would not be stopped by her, nor myself.

When she took me in her arms and held me, I felt
the most sincere, genuine, and honest hug from her. In my
mind, it was as if the hug lasted for an hour, but I know it
lasted but moments. When we let go, she smiled and said,
"Welcome." Right there, IT BEGAN. I watched her and all
of the volunteers that weekend show us all such kindness
while wanting nothing in return; I watched them speak of
a God they loved so passionately. I wanted to know that
passion.

— James

A number of years ago, I became a certified recovery coach
through the Connecticut Community of Addiction and
Recovery (CCAR), which is nationally recognized as one of the
leading recovery coach training programs. The course manual
was about 170 pages, only two or three of which concerned spiritual wellness. We were told spiritual wellness wasn't a significant
component of recovery. In our increasingly secular culture, this
may not come as much of a surprise.

Yet of the seventeen people taking the class that day, fourteen were themselves in long-term recovery, and thirteen of
those fourteen spoke to me personally about the role of a spiritual awakening in their journeys. This spiritual awakening that
kept them clean, that gave their lives meaning and purpose, was
what had brought them to that very room. But the course that
would certify us as recovery coaches — that would prepare and
establish us to mentor and walk with people through the journey of recovery — indicated that spirituality, in this context, was
taboo.

The global and secular National Wellness Institute professes quite the opposite. Its time-tested definition of wellness is "an active process through which people become aware of, and make choices toward, a more successful existence."[1] The framework to help people achieve this status is the institute's interdependent model, the Six Dimensions of Wellness: emotional, occupational, physical, social, intellectual, and spiritual. All dimensions are necessary for an "evolving process of achieving full potential" and ultimately for living with "a holistic sense of wellness and fulfillment."[2] So why the disconnect with the clinical world?

Misconceptions

Too often, spirituality is misinterpreted as religiosity. To speak of spirituality is presumed to be proselytizing, and that presumption alone can cause programs to lose the government money they need to survive. Clinical treatment programs are also wary of the potential to offend by hinting at spirituality.

In 2016, I was asked to give a session on spirituality at a Christian-run community-based residential treatment facility for those who are addicted to drugs and alcohol. I prepared my presentation, gathered song sheets for the hundred people who would be there, and so on. Before I began, the clinical director who'd invited me pulled me aside and asked me to do her a favor: "Don't mention God."

I was incredulous. This was a spirituality session at a Christian facility, and I was being told I couldn't talk about God.

I got around it by speaking through the prism of my own experience, in the vein of "I don't know what this will look like for you, but my higher power — whom I choose to call God — repaired me in my brokenness." As long as I framed it through the lens of my experience, it wasn't a problem. Still, I was left shaking my head.

Thank God at least non-denominational spirituality sessions have come into greater favor since then, and certainly in the midst of the pandemic. We have come to be in greater need of figuring out why we're here, of articulating our purpose. We can't get that from anything other than the development of spiritual life. More and more, people who can share a concept of spirituality and help people find that for themselves are being recognized as important. One of these people is needed wherever someone needs to be accompanied — in other words, everywhere.

Action taken out of fear is always inferior to action chosen out of love and charity. Jesus, of course, was never afraid of offending. Scripture teaches that "if any one has the world's goods and sees his brother in need, yet closes his heart against him, how does God's love abide in him?" (1 Jn 3:17). Here, the fear of transgressing a cultural boundary shuts the door on a dimension of wellness that could lend purpose, meaning, and so much more to someone's life.

I always tell the people I meet in detox and long-term treatment facilities that I am not interested in their being clean and sober. That usually causes some raised eyebrows — until I tell them that I want *more* for them. In John 10:10, Jesus says, "I came that they may have life, and have it abundantly." I want them to have an abundant life. I want them to have joy, peace, happiness, fulfillment. In short, I want them to live the lives they were created to live.

Not using alcohol or drugs is not enough, and frankly, often such abstinence doesn't last. To incorporate spirituality into recovery is to invite people to abundance, to initiate them into something that will give them joy and serenity. There simply isn't a substitute for spirituality. It is ludicrous not to acknowledge, if not really advocate for, spirituality as a necessary dimension of a human being's wellness.

Spirituality: The Key to Recovery?

I wholeheartedly believe in the one, holy, Catholic, and apostolic Church and in our Mother Church's desire and ability to provide spiritually for the sick and suffering. I can also speak in terms that can meet people where they are.

Bill Wilson, acknowledged co-founder of Alcoholics Anonymous, always knew that God needed to be part of the recovery equation. He accepted that the people his program would serve had a range of experiences with faith. Some would be Christians, others atheists, and still others followers of other religions. This spiritual range is why the Twelve Steps speak of a "higher power" or "the God of your understanding" rather than God the Father and the Holy Trinity. In reflecting on the development of the program, Wilson said, "God was certainly there in our Steps, but He was now expressed in terms that anybody — *anybody at all* — could accept and try."[3]

But the spiritual concept remains at the heart of the program; spirituality is key to recovery. Wilson knew then something that we're trying to prove today; namely, that it's imperative for those in recovery to develop an intimacy with a power greater than themselves to restore them to sanity. That may seem a flippant way to put it, but "wellness" or "health" originates in the Latin root *sanus*, from which the English language derives the word "sane."

Programs supported by the government have their hands tied when it comes to spirituality. Faith communities, then, need to get more involved. When faith communities talk about spirituality in the right way — in an inclusive way, in a way that responds to brokenness and sets out a path to spiritual healing — it does so much good. You would be amazed at how many secular organizations call me in to speak about spirituality. Those walking with folks in recovery are seeing the need for it, but clinical treatment, on its own, doesn't adequately provide it. We need to step in and fill that gap.

Four years ago, I met a young Jewish woman from Livingston, New Jersey. When she was seventeen years old, she lost a classmate to an overdose. Her school ignored the reality of the heroin problem in their community, perhaps because they were ashamed, perhaps because they didn't know how to deal with it. She and the other young adults were bereft. The powers that be may have thought they were protecting someone — themselves? — but actually, they were neglecting the young people's grief, which only hurt them more.

Then a rabbi held a service for the kids who had known this young man. All of them went, even those who had left the practice of Judaism. They went because they needed it. They weren't getting the support, the comfort, the act of accompaniment from the secular world. When someone offered them compassion from a place of faith — even when they wouldn't have sought a place of worship on their own — they flocked to the comfort and empathy for which they so desperately thirsted. These young people underscored the need for deep spiritual healing in the face of this great tragedy, a spiritual healing that our Catholic Church can and should provide.

We need to love like Jesus and welcome everyone who comes to us with the same dignity and respect. Many of our brothers and sisters have not been taught about the love of God, so they seek fulfillment in what they know. One man described it to me as always feeling like a square peg in a round hole.

It is up to us to point the way to the only One who can satisfy that desire, even as we travel that road ourselves. In the state of the current societal malady of substance use disorders, the Catholic Church can meet the needs of her own flock while being a model for other faith communities to follow.

The Opioid Crisis: How Did We Get Here?

It's natural to want to understand how our brothers and sisters came to depend so heavily on the chemicals that dictate their lives. Although this book offers a useful framework for understanding and responding to any substance use or addiction disorder, much of the discussion centers on the opioid epidemic. Opioids are unique, in that many who are afflicted are specifically plagued with iatrogenic opioid dependence. "Iatrogenic" simply means they were legitimately prescribed opioids for pain as part of medical treatment and subsequently became addicted.

The addictive properties of opioids have been ignored and denied for as long as they've existed. Beth Macy masterfully chronicles the rise of opioid use in her book *Dopesick: Dealers, Doctors, and the Drug Company That Addicted America* (the inspiration for the Hulu miniseries with the same name). She notes how the inventor of morphine himself urged caution in 1810, how Richmond doctor W. G. Rogers "demanded prompt action to curb the rampant use of opioids in 1884," and how the Harrison Narcotics Act of 1914 "severely restricted the sale and possession of heroin and other narcotic drugs" (because at the turn of the century, heroin was available for purchase at drug stores) — all before Dr. Art Van Zee and Sister Beth Davies "sound[ed] the first sentinel alarm from Appalachia" in 2000.[4] It's no secret that opiates and opioids are addictive, even in doses that are initially small and limited. It's also no secret that their addictive nature means a great deal of money can be made in their licit and illicit sale.

OxyContin, the brand name for oxycodone, was approved by the Food and Drug Administration in late 1995. By 2001, "doctors, hospitals, and accreditation boards were adopting the notion of pain as 'the fifth vital sign' [giving] pain equal status with blood pressure, heart rate, respiratory rate, and temperature" when making assessments and determining treatment plans.[5] In her book *Drug Dealer, MD: How Doctors Were Duped, Patients Got Hooked and Why It's So Hard to Stop*, Anna Lembke, MD, professor of psychiatry at Stanford University School of Medicine and chief of the Stanford Addiction Medicine Dual Diagnosis Clinic, writes, "Two hundred years ago, physical pain was viewed by most physicians as a desirable component of the healing process."[6] Pain management became a discipline unto itself by the 1950s, "driven by refined technology that allowed for opioids to be readily synthesized in the laboratory and by an efficient pharmaceutical industry eager to sell them."[7]

Today, she says, "doctors who leave pain untreated are not just demonstrating poor clinical skills; they are viewed as morally compromised" and "legally liable for malpractice."[8] No scientific studies have proven that the pain scale used to assess this fifth vital sign "correlates with improved patient outcomes"; studies do show, however, that "use of these pain scores increases opioid prescribing and opioid use."[9]

Never before were opioids prescribed for a tooth pull. Never before were opioids used in circumstances outside of palliative and end-of-life care. Now, OxyContin was being marketed inappropriately and ineffectively for all degrees and kinds of pain. Salespeople targeted geographical regions dominated by low-income populations who were susceptible to pain as a work hazard; for example, West Virginia coal miners.

Macy writes that Purdue Pharma, the marketing arm of family-owned pharmaceutical company Purdue Frederick, quickly "touted the safety of its new opioid-delivery system everywhere its merchants went," telling doctors across the country that, because it was time-released, when used properly, the risk of addiction was less than one-half of one percent.[10] This claim was later proven to have been false advertising in the very worst way — Macy cites the actual number as high as 56 percent — but not before thousands upon thousands of people lost their livelihoods and their lives to this drug and other related medications to which many desperate users were led.[11]

Purdue Pharma put its all into making sure doctors would prescribe its latest drug. Sales-rep bonuses were $1 million in 1996; they rose to $40 million in 2001, just five years later. These bonuses trickled down to the prescribing doctors. They didn't always understand what they were prescribing — or over-prescribing. What they did know was that they were getting a cut each time they wrote a script for this new-to-the-market drug. Doctors were invited to all-expenses-paid conferences in resort atmospheres. They received all manner of compensation for prescribing Oxy — meals, gas in their cars, Christmas trees, and more. Meanwhile, those who had become addicted were broke and became willing to do anything to obtain enough of the drug to feel normal. Emmit Yeary, a lawyer who represented those facing criminal retribution for Oxy-related crimes, said, "The irony of it was, the victims were getting jail time instead of the people who caused it."[12]

Lembke believes:

> To ascribe all the blame to Big Pharma is to oversimplify. The pharmaceutical industry was able to influence doctor-prescribing only by joining together with academic physicians, professional medical societies, regulatory agencies (the Federation of State Medical Boards and The Joint Commission), and the Food and Drug Administration. Together, these different factions manipulated and misrepresented, deliberately or otherwise, medical science to serve their own agendas.[13]

Why did the opioid epidemic take so long to make headlines, if so many people were getting sick, getting arrested, dying? Van Zee watched the crisis unfold before his eyes among his friends in his rural Virginia county — the poorest county in the state — and he was one of the first to put the pieces together. The statistics had to reach the suburbs and the cities before anyone with a loud enough voice took notice.[14] Once people in places of power started to understand what was going on, the additional problem was that, as Macy aptly points out, "the legal and medical structures meant to combat America's heroin epidemic were woefully disconnected, often at odds with one another, and full of unintended consequences."[15]

No one at the beginning thought this new medication would initiate such a tornado of a disease, affecting multiple generations.

Dealing with this onslaught of addiction in every community, eventually in every state, every town, has not been part of clergy formation. Priests and bishops have not been prepared to deal with it. But if we can understand addiction as a spiritual disease of unnatural attachment, we can see it more clearly for what it is. We can see it through the lens of Scripture, through teachings we already know, and we can see that, in fact, we are all equipped to deal with it in our own ways.

This Is Your Brain on Drugs

To appreciate how spirituality plays into addiction, we also need to understand the physiology of addiction. Lembke describes addiction as "an altered brain state in which motivation for basic survival has been 'hijacked' by the drive to obtain and use substances."[16] Whether the addiction is chemical (drugs, alcohol) or behavioral (gambling, sex), changes in brain chemistry work in basically the same way, though chemical addiction creates a greater urgency.

Drugs, alcohol, and addictive behaviors all cause the brain to flood with dopamine, which disrupts the normal communication that happens in this all-important organ of the body.

Dopamine stimulates feelings of pleasure, which the brain naturally craves. The body wants and then needs more and more dopamine to experience the same euphoria. Eventually the brain stops producing its own dopamine, becoming entirely dependent on the substance or behavior and always-increasing amounts of it.

Without the object of the addiction, the person doesn't know how to feel normal anymore, because the brain chemistry has undergone an unnatural transformation. I've worked with people who need thirty bags of heroin each day just to feel the way you and I do when we wake up each morning. This increasing threshold is why someone addicted to drugs or alcohol can't "just stop." The real, physiological pain that results from abrupt disuse of a substance to which one has been addicted for a length of time is incredible.

For opioid use, the physical dimension of withdrawal, often referred to as "dopesickness," can present with "nausea, diarrhea, insomnia, irritability, anxiety, and painful muscle cramps — the last being the origin of the phrase 'kicking the habit.'"[17] A woman interviewed in *Dopesick* put it this way: "You ache so bad and you're so irritable that you can't stand to be touched. Your legs shake so bad you can't sleep. You're as ill as one hornet could ever be. ... And believe me, you'll do anything to make that pain go away."[18]

The biological reality is that the brain of the addicted person can't do what it used to do on its own anymore. A person suffering from addiction looking for the next fix is not necessarily seeking a recreational high. Even those who want to get better reach a point at which "this pain is so intense and overwhelming that it compels repeat drug use, not to feel high but just to equilibrate the beam and feel normal."[19] Lembke also highlights the simultaneous "emotional pain of protracted psychological withdrawal ... which can go on for weeks, months, and in some cases, years."[20]

Those addicted to drugs and alcohol often come to suffer as well from lung and cardiovascular disease, stroke, cancers, HIV/AIDS, and mental health issues (which may have led to the substance use disorder or which may have been brought on or exacerbated by the disorder). People afflicted with addiction get strange maladies and infections, too. I remember sitting in the hospital emergency room with John as the nurses and doctors swarmed around him to respond to the terrible case of cellulitis he had developed in his legs. Once the veins in his arms collapsed, he started shooting up between his toes.

We need to understand that when an addiction has been formed, the afflicted person is not making conscious choices, though it feels that way to those around them. Can you imagine any other disease where parents give up their children, where a man would choose a substance over his wife? How many times have family members said to me, "If she loved her kids enough, she would just stop"? Frustrated and jaded family members often can't understand that addiction compromises one's freedom. It's not that the battle can't be won, but the person in long-term recovery must always thereafter be conscious of the temptation to capitulate to the pull of their former attachment.

What looks like choosing a substance over a relationship is actually a reflection of a physiological need. The choice is not part of the person that you know, not the behavior of the one you love. So on one end of the relationship, it's a very personal hurt.

What makes everything even more challenging is that addiction itself is incompatible with true spiritual growth. The unnatural attachment to substance or behavior — recall that image of me with my hand right in front of my face, from chapter 1 — makes impossible a relationship with the Lord, that space in which someone suffering from any other disease can find transformation and redemptive suffering. Whereas someone battling cancer can be drawn into deeper communion with the Lord, a person afflicted with substance use disorder can't make those connections because they're still perseverating on the object of their attachment. All he can see is what it's going to take to feel some semblance of his own distorted normalcy.

"I Never Thought to Call the Church"

My parish priest called me one day after daily Mass and said, "There's someone here you know how to help more than I do."

I got in my car and drove back to my church. Inside, I found a thirty-seven-year-old woman addicted to heroin, sitting next to her father. Missy[21] was the mother of a son who had passed away at age seventeen from a debilitating neurological disease, akin to ALS for kids. When his disease progressed, she had to do an enormous amount of hard physical labor in caring for him, despite the back issues she had developed in caring for her other child, a wheelchair-bound daughter with cerebral palsy. She was prescribed opiates for the resulting pain, and when her prescription ran out after a number of years, she turned to street drugs. Today at the church, she was ready to look for help. I sent her father and priest out of the room and talked with her.

Missy hadn't used since the day before, and I could see she was going into early withdrawal. By the grace of God, I got her into a detox facility in Port Jervis, New York. I drove her there and then sat with her in the ER, praying the Rosary as we waited for the detox bed to open. When the staff were about to take her upstairs, Missy turned to me and said, "Can you call my mother and let her know where I am?"

She gave me the number and I made the call. I told Missy's mom she was in detox and recounted how she'd gotten there.

Her mother replied, "I can't thank you enough. I never thought to call the Church."

In a way, this was mind-blowing to me. The Church is supposed to be a koinonia, a community, a fellowship, a communion. We are called to serve one another. But then, I am also keenly aware that, as a Church, we haven't done a good job of redirecting people back to us, largely because we don't understand these societal maladies.

The Church has to be able to provide resources, compassion, and companionship. And then we need to let people *know* we are a resource. When we do, we will heal the Church as well as the individuals participating.

As I mentioned earlier in this chapter, the clinical continuum of care currently recommended for addicted persons doesn't include a spiritual element. From detox to treatment facility, from halfway house to sober living house, rarely does anyone help those in either early or long-term recovery grow in the spiritual life.

People need a space to be able to safely say, "I'm angry at God. Can you help me?" Or, "I was baptized and I want to understand how God fits into my life, how my life fits into God's love." Those fielding these questions at the parish or diocesan level don't need to have answers. They only need to be open to being companions. May put it well: "What is not needed is saintliness but honesty, compassion, good common sense, and the ability to listen."[22]

A while back, I met a woman whose grown son was an alcoholic. She was filled with such worry and concern over him and his children. Her family and siblings were tired of listening to her talk about her son. She made an appointment with me, and we met at a coffee shop.

For an hour and a half, she talked. I listened attentively with a straw in my mouth, sipping an iced tea. I didn't say more than ten words in those ninety minutes. When she finally came up for air, she said it was the best session she'd had. And it wasn't because I offered her anything more than what Pope Francis calls the "apostolate of the ear: listening before speaking."[23] I simply made space for her, and I listened to all that she felt had gone unheard. To be honest, it wasn't a big ask. But it also wasn't something she had found anywhere else.

This spiritual connection, this vulnerability, this gift of time, and this lack of judgment — those afflicted and their friends and family so desperately need all of these things in order to start on the road to healing. People need to be seen; they need to be loved. This doesn't take some advanced training or certification. It only means recognizing that human beings are mind, body, and soul and that each of those has inherent dignity, no matter what decisions have been made. We need to see this reality and accept it, to feel it deeply enough within ourselves to start taking action, for the good of their souls and our own.

Reflect

- Many people believe that addiction is a person's choice, without understanding the mitigating physiological and psychological factors that keep a person enslaved. How would you explain the mind-body-spirit connection of this disease to someone who wonders why people can't "just stop"?
- Our spirituality gives meaning and purpose to our lives, as we seek to live in love and service to our brothers and sisters. How has your spiritual life led to your personal joy, serenity, and abundance?
- Pope Francis calls the act of accompanying someone by attentive listening "the apostolate of the ear." How has your attentive listening to someone been a blessing in his or her life? How has someone's attentive listening to you been a blessing in your own life?

Pray

Merciful God and Father, give us the strength to carry the message of your unending love and mercy to those who have been burdened by the weight of their addictions.

Let us never fear rejection, for it is in our rejection by others that we draw closest to you, who was more rejected than all others.

Fortify us so that we might have the courage to fight the injustices of the world, especially those injustices caused by the greed of those who prey upon the vulnerable and the marginalized.

As your hands and feet in this sorrowful world, let us toil to bring your kingdom on earth as it is in heaven for the good of all your children.

Amen.

3
These Least Brothers and Sisters of Mine

As far back as I can remember, all I wanted was to love and be loved. To my dismay, most of the people I encountered in life didn't have that same energy, primarily my parents. I couldn't figure out why I was this way, and felt weird and weak for the love I so wanted to give, but wasn't reciprocated.

As a result of not knowing how to cope with so much rejection and abandonment, I spiraled into the miserable, lonely world of alcoholism. I had been committed to asylums, put in jail, and near death on more than a few occasions. It wasn't until I felt soulless that I finally cried out to God for help. Once in treatment, I got to the root of a lot of my troubles. I discovered that the love I'd so wanted to express was in fact my greatest strength. I also discovered that I'm most fulfilled when helping others.

And now, at over five years sober, I'm in New Jersey, with arms wide open, helping whoever I can, whenever possible. Thank you, God, for the ability to still love, and for granting me this wonderful opportunity. It turns out, I am my brothers' and sisters' keeper.

— Mosadi-Rra

For too long, we as a Church have acted as either the priest or the Levite in the story of the Good Samaritan. In the story from the Gospel of Luke, a man has been stripped, beaten, and left half-dead by robbers on the road from Jerusalem to Jericho. A priest and a Levite see this sick and suffering man on their journeys, but both choose to pass him by on the opposite side of the road. Perhaps you've heard the cultural context in a homily at some point. At that time, they believed that if they were to touch the man, they would be considered unclean and unable to participate in religious offerings. They don't want to get messy. They don't want to be inconvenienced, and they avoid him for a purpose they can justify to themselves as worthy.

But the Samaritan, "as he journeyed, came to where he was; and when he saw him, he had compassion" (Lk 10:33). In this culture, Samaritans themselves were looked down upon; the scholar of the law and the crowd listening to Christ relate this parable would have expected little of the Samaritan. And yet Jesus says it was the Samaritan who "went to him and bound up his wounds, pouring on oil and wine; then he set him on his own beast and brought him to an inn, and took care of him. And the next day he took out two denarii and gave them to the innkeeper, saying, 'Take care of him; and whatever more you spend, I will repay you when I come back'" (Lk 10:34–35).

Even the listening scholar of the law, whose intent was to test the Lord, could articulate that the right thing to do in this situation was to show the man mercy. Jesus responds simply, saying to him, "Go and do likewise" (Lk 10:37).

These are my marching orders. I take them directly from Christ. We are called to get messy, to touch the blood of the victim, to do that which repels us. Many people don't know where to start with ministering to addicted people and to their friends and family, so they don't start at all. We, as the Church, have a sound understanding of what it is to be human, of what it is to be broken and what it takes to be made whole again. We know forgiveness and redemption. We have hope in the promise of Jesus Christ, risen. We have an obligation to share this message with those who need it.

We need to respond, then, to those who are treated as modern-day lepers by offering charitable action, by making spiritual and corporal acts of mercy. We need to look to see the face of Christ in each of the sick and suffering and in their family members, who are often in the background, often unseen, but suffering just the same. We need to dispel the myth of the "other."

The Treasures of the Church
In an August 2019 talk, Pope Francis called the early Church "a 'field hospital' that welcomes the weakest, that is, the sick" and encouraged the faithful to respond to the suffering: "The sick are privileged for the Church, for the priestly heart, for all the faithful. They are not to be discarded. On the contrary, they are to be healed, to be cared for. They are the object of Christian concern."[1]

His words recall a famous line from Saint Lawrence (I was born on this saint's feast day, so I feel a special connection to him). In the year 258, shortly after the beheading of Pope Sixtus, Saint Lawrence was charged by Emperor Valerian to hand over all the treasures of the Church. Saint Lawrence had been made archdeacon of Rome, which meant he was in charge of the Church's assets. Three days later, Saint Lawrence appeared before the emperor with the blind, poor, crippled, and suffering people of Rome. "These," Saint Lawrence declared, "are the true treasures of the Church."[2] This statement is as true today, nearly two thousand years later. It is in serving the sick and suffering, in seeing them, in accompanying them on their journeys that we live as Christ's hands and feet.

When I was first getting started in this ministry, I mentioned my work to a priest with whom I wasn't familiar. I asked if his parish offered resources for addicted persons and their families. I've had this conversation many times over the years, with lay people as well as clergy. Today, more and more priests and deacons understand that they need to know more about resources for those dealing with addiction. More are participating in iTHIRST and coming to this understanding.

But at the time, my exchange with this priest was not uncommon.

When I asked him about addicted persons, he responded that people were making their own choices. He believed substance use disorder to be a moral failing. His particular perspective simultaneously misunderstood the disease of addiction and discarded the totality of the human person.

I knew his observations weren't true, but I found another way in. "Isn't that our gig anyway?" I asked. "Aren't we supposed to reach out to our brothers and sisters who go down the wrong moral path, or suffer from spiritual sickness, or whatever you want to call it? There's nothing you can call it that diminishes our responsibility to respond."

I don't share this anecdote to look down on clergy in general, of course. So many deacons, priests, bishops, and cardinals appreciate the gravity of the situation and understand the need for all of us Christians to step up. Lay people and clergy need to work together to serve those in our "field hospital." Our common baptism anointed all of us as members of the Church to be priest, prophet, and king. We are all called by Christ himself to undertake this dirty, smelly, unpolished, unfiltered service.

In another instance early in this ministry, I was in daily Mass on a Tuesday morning. I admit I was zoning out a little. I was talking with God, praying, "Okay, this ministry is happening. What am I supposed to do with it?"

I know the answer came from God and not from my own brain, because it was very simple.

"Show them how much I love them," I heard him say.

"Okay," I responded. I could do that.

We can do that.

How We Can Show God's Love

To this day, my mission remains the same: that somehow through our work, people who didn't know it before will come to know how much Christ loves them — especially people who are vulnerable, people who have been marginalized. This mission means seeing in each addicted person a unique and irreplaceable child of God. Each person has a story. Each person has a life worth living. Substance use disorders transcend age, gender, religion, socioeconomic background, professional status, and so much else. To respond in love means not generalizing or condescending. We need to listen with the intention of understanding how the person afflicted with addiction got to this point from wherever she was before. This listening in itself is a too-often neglected act of mercy.

The way to start is simple: Just be kind. My own little church in the woods has an Alcoholics Anonymous meeting once a week. On a snowy Saturday morning, I had business at the church, as I was directing a service project for a local halfway house, collecting toiletries, socks, underwear, and other items for Christmas.

The AA meeting broke up, and people began exiting from the side room they used. I met some of the people as they walked by and simply welcomed them to the parish, saying, "You are as welcome in the sanctuary as you are in that small room."

One fellow replied, "I'm Jewish, but that was the nicest welcome, and maybe someday I'll come to join you." It was a great moment, a moment of embrace, and it took only a few seconds.

I would love every church to host Twelve Step recovery meetings like Alcoholics Anonymous and Narcotics Anonymous (for those struggling with addiction) and Al-Anon and Nar-Anon (for those who love someone struggling with addiction). I understand that these groups hold their meetings in side rooms and basements in order to protect the anonymity of the participants. But I'd also like to find a way to let participants know they are welcome "up top" too, in whatever way they feel comfortable. When we strive to see others as God sees them — as his children, each with unique and irreplaceable dignity — we can love them as he does. We can engage with them. We can invite them to help us form a ministry that tends to the totality of the person.

Tapping into the Theology of the Body

If we are true disciples, we need to be able to look at someone society has given up on or thrown away and recognize in them the face of Christ. We need to see a person of unique human dignity. We need to love them when they can't love themselves. The Catholic point of view understands mind, body, and spirit as being inextricably linked. Jesuit theologian and paleontologist Pierre Teilhard de Chardin said, "We are not human beings having a spiritual experience. We are spiritual beings having a human experience."[3]

In the series of audiences in which he developed his Theology of the Body, Pope St. John Paul II elaborated on the impossibility of dissociating body from spirit as we strive to honor the unique human dignity of every person. As human beings, we are perfect combinations of body and spirit, and the gift of our faith is the understanding of the connection of all parts. The popular understanding of the Theology of the Body limits it to teachings on sexuality, marriage, and family, but it is so much more than that. It means recognizing the personhood of every child of God.

Fr. Zachary Swantek, chaplain and director of the Aquinas Institute for Catholic Life at Princeton University, holds a licentiate (S.T.L.) from the John Paul II Institute for Studies on Marriage and Family. Father Zack says it's crucial to remind those struggling with addiction of their dignity and of their very humanity:

> They are loved, both loved by God but also loved through that encounter with another person, because we're meant for communion that's formed through mutual self-gift. The greatest expression of that [self-gift] is through marriage and family, but it's not limited to that. All the time we're meant to give of ourselves in different ways, and especially for the vulnerable person, for the sick person, for the addicted person, [so] that somebody can see their dignity, even if they [themselves] don't see it, and continue to give of themself out of love for that person, even when it seems ugly or dark.[4]

When another person freely chooses to love and accompany the person who is vulnerable, sick, or addicted — even when it means seeing the worst in the person — "the person's attitude about himself can little by little change, where they start to see this as this opportunity to remember that they're not meant to be this way," explains Father Zack. The one who was guilt-ridden and ashamed "can start breaking through and starting to want to respond to the gift that's received."

You may have noticed that I do not use "addict" as a noun (although some quoted passages might), nor will I for the remainder of this book. We cannot use a label to objectify our brothers and sisters suffering from this spiritual disease. We must not see afflicted persons as "other." We need to see each one of them as God our Father sees them. In charity and mercy, we are charged with helping every one of them realize the same in themselves.

We are called to first recognize our own vulnerability and humility, so we can accept that "God continues to love us and continues to reach out to us and see the dignity we've been created for and that we're loved now, not when we get our act together and everything's perfect," says Father Zack. We then have an obligation to share that love with others. Father Zack says we need to be "like Jesus when he encounters people who have gotten trapped by sin or through sickness," seeing how "he's able to recognize the dignity of the person there whom he created and invite them out of that ... to rediscover their freedom and dignity."

The shame that often comes with addiction can certainly be isolating, but Father Zack indicates that, through the lens of the Theology of the Body, shame "can also be this boundary experience that pushes us, points us back to the beginning, to how we were created to be." It helps us realize "that we're not meant to be alone, but we're meant to be in the Father's house, or we're meant to be in communion with others."

The Catholic Church teaches the truth about free will, human nature, human dignity, and what real freedom is. "We cannot understand how to help people if we have a false understanding of our humanity, and what our fulfillment is, and what freedom is, and what dignity is, so we need that real adequate anthropology of what it means to be created in the image and likeness of God," Father Zack explains. Again, we can see how this mission is rooted in Scripture, how we are called to heal through encounter in the same way that Jesus did.

Each human being is a gift from God, a soul with whom God desires to spend all eternity. When we encounter a soul in need — and Father Zack deftly acknowledges that we're all going to encounter these souls, whether at work, at school, in our families, or elsewhere in our communities — we ought to ask ourselves, "How is God calling me to make this gift of myself for their own good and taking their good as my own good?"

Foremost, we need to pray, says Father Zack, recalling the words of Jesus in John 15:5: "I am the vine, you are the branches. He who abides in me, and I in him, he it is that bears much fruit, for apart from me you can do nothing." He recommends "praying especially for the Church and its members to recognize this missionary mandate that we have."

Then we must invite people into our churches, our communities, and our families. We, as a Church, can give people something others can't: the look of love we all naturally crave. Pope Emeritus Benedict XVI wrote in *Deus Caritas Est* that this "seeing with the eyes of Christ" is only possible "on the basis of an intimate encounter with God, an encounter which has become a communion of will."[5] Through prayer, worship, and the sacraments, Father Zack says, "The more that we can look at people, see them the way that Christ sees," the more "they can see Christ in us, and we can see Christ suffering in them."

The Theology of the Body can help us realize, as a Church, that we have a responsibility to those who are suffering, even when their behaviors are deplorable. This theology can help those suffering be open to healing. And it can serve as our natural call to action to serve these brothers and sisters of ours. In serving, we who do not directly suffer can recognize our own dignity as children of God. Father Zack highlights that Pope St. John Paul II acknowledged providing this adequate anthropology and applying it to marital love and God's plan, yet encouraged us to apply it to many other things, especially suffering and death, which Father Zack notes "is so important to the Biblical message."

"*Gloria enim Dei vivens homo, vita autem hominis visio Dei,*" wrote Saint Iraneus. "For the glory of God is the living man, and the life of man is the vision of God." We are called to be that vision, to give of ourselves in the same way Christ gave himself for us on the cross. In *Gaudium et Spes*, Pope St. Paul VI wrote:

> God, who has fatherly concern for everyone, has willed that all men should constitute one family and treat one another in a spirit of brotherhood. … [Jesus] implied a certain likeness between the union of the divine Persons, and the unity of God's sons in truth and charity. This likeness reveals that man, who is the only creature on earth which God willed for itself, cannot fully find himself except through a sincere gift of himself.[6]

God willing, after all the obstacles, fear, doubt, and shame are stripped away, we will see the sick and suffering among us emerge into their authentic selves. This experience is one of the greatest blessings of this messy and challenging work. How beautiful it would be if our Church — remember, the Church is us — would willingly open her arms to them and recognize the treasures they are.

Reflect

- The parable of the Good Samaritan reminds us that it is easy to pass by those whose lives have become messy. Yet Jesus commands us to be merciful like the Samaritan was, when he says, "Go and do likewise." Have you ever felt passed over by someone who might have been in a position to assist you? How did that make you feel?
- We are called upon as Christians to spread Christ's love and mercy to all we meet and to realize the unique human dignity of every person, no matter his station in life. How can ministering to those on the peripheries help us understand Saint Lawrence's

concept of the "treasures of the Church" in the twenty-first century?

- Beyond teaching about human sexuality, marriage, and family, Pope St. John Paul II's Theology of the Body encourages us to recognize how God calls us to make a gift of ourselves to others. How have you experienced the gift of another person through encounter? In what way can you deepen your appreciation of others' unique human dignity, through this "real adequate anthropology of what it means to be created in the image and likeness of God," and then respond to someone in need this week?

Pray

Dear Lord, fill me with your mercy and compassion, so that I may never pass by a brother or sister in need, but act the way of the Good Samaritan in caring for all those who suffer.

Open my eyes so that, like Saint Lawrence, I may recognize that those whom society has cast away, the least of these, are in fact the ones whom you draw closest to your heart, the true treasures of the Church.

Help me to see that every human life, born or unborn, was created in your image and likeness and possesses a unique human dignity that cannot be denied by any other person.

Holy Spirit, set my heart aflame, so that in true Christian love, I might serve all those who are vulnerable and marginalized and, in so doing, fulfill your words from the Gospel of Matthew, "Whatever you did for one of these least brothers of mine, you did for me."

Amen.

4

Out of Darkness and Into the Light

During my active addiction, there were moments when I stumbled around, refusing help and doing things my way. As a result, I repeatedly injured myself and hurt those in my family who were doing their best to love me.

It reminds me of the times I have walked into a dark room to retrieve an item, without turning on the light switch. I justify this poor decision because I am absolutely certain of where each piece of furniture is located and have entered this room thousands of times before. Undoubtedly, I knock over a lamp or stub my toe (again) on a table leg. If a well-meaning member of my family asks me if I need help, I am aggravated by their offer. Of course I don't need help! I know exactly what I'm doing! The solu-

tion to my problem seems obvious to everyone else: Just turn on the light!

The dynamic between someone with addiction and a family member can be similar. Sometimes it's the addict who is lost in the darkness, annoyed by offers of help and words of concern. At other times, the family of the afflicted is stubbornly ignoring the obvious, unwilling or unable to just "turn on the light" and recognize they also need help.

— Deirdre

The mission of iTHIRST is to empower priests, deacons, religious, and lay people — in a word, the Church — to become a resource for those suffering from addictions and for their families. Wherever the Catholic Church exists, be it a school, hospital, or parish, someone needs to be ready when an individual knocks at the door for help with a substance use disorder. Someone needs to be prepared to say, "We understand how you got there, and we are here to welcome you home, back to Christ."

The ITSCs I train are not spiritual directors but pilgrims, people who are likewise on the journey, albeit steadier on their feet. The role of the ITSC is to prayerfully help another soul respond to the promptings of the Holy Spirit, so that they can make better choices based on those promptings, beyond the prism of their own experiences.

The level of power between the two companions is identical. Each must be aware of their own spiritual condition. There is a necessary self-emptying. We need to sweep out the trash in our outer rooms, so that we have room for Christ in our interior room. When we get rid of our false sense of self, we find God in his indwelling within ourselves. It's only when we give our fiat to walking that journey that we develop a deeper intimacy with the Lord. We are called to listen from a place of hope, to listen with love in our hearts.

It's no newsflash that our cultural conversation hinges on soundbites and headlines, offenses taken without context. We have forgotten how to listen properly, and this is a travesty for those suffering. Listening is a skill we need to learn — or relearn. It's something we're all capable of. Pope Francis writes, "Listening means paying attention, wanting to understand, to value, to respect and to ponder what the other person says."[1] When we encounter someone in difficulty, the pope encourages standing beside them and listening. "Don't say: 'I have the solution for you.' No, as a friend, slowly give them strength by your words, give them strength by your listening, that medicine which sadly is being forgotten: 'the therapy of listening.'"[2]

Discerning a Better Way

The ITSC training, what I often refer to as "the curriculum," is the end product of a journey that began in 2016, when I had a very different idea of what this was going to be.

For two years, I'd been working with the recovery retreat ministry at Trinity House at the Shrine of St. Joseph, a mission site of the Missionary Servants of the Most Holy Trinity, a Catholic community of priests and brothers established by Fr. Thomas Augustine Judge. It had become evident to the retreat team that the Church and the ministry needed to do more to work with those who were suffering. The weekend retreats went so well that we had the idea of establishing a sanctuary through the Missionary Servants, one where individuals could come for that kind of spiritual retreat for a longer period of time — two weeks, or even four weeks. In that space, we would have the time to imbue them with the Holy Spirit, to shower them with love, and to restore their unique human dignity.

I found the perfect spot just ten minutes from my house. It was a beautiful but abandoned Marian shrine. A priest had built it years ago, and we were going to make it a sober-living community. We'd call it Mercy House. We had courses and schedules. We would house twelve people at a time. We'd make an intentional practice of our spirituality. We had an advisory board going already. And we'd have Mass every day. We met on a Thursday to formalize the lease, and the plan was for the current owners to review and sign it shortly thereafter.

Then the whole thing fell through. It was utterly wiped out. For a few days, the owner, the niece of the priest who'd built it, wouldn't respond to us.

That Sunday, September 11, 2016, we got a one-liner from her that said she didn't think her uncle would have agreed with our mission.

I went ballistic. I was crushed. I'd thought this property was the answer to all my prayers.

A few weeks later, on Tuesday, October 4, 2016, I went to daily Mass. I was angry with our Blessed Mother. "You got us this far," I told her. "How could you let the evil one stop this?"

In a mystical experience, I simply heard her say, "I didn't let the evil one; I stopped this."

When I asked why, she said, "Because you need to do this first."

I looked up at the crucifix and heard "I THIRST." I knew it was an acronym. I heard it. What we were planning to do with the Marian shrine wasn't enough. We needed programs for education and prevention. We needed support for the incarcerated and for those in treatment. We needed aftercare and community -building support. I ran home and created a two-page document that outlined what would become everything.

I drove to Paterson to see Br. Joe Dudek, ST, who was my mentor and the Missionary Servant in charge of the retreat program. I told him, "I know why everything stopped. This is what we have to do."

He replied, "I don't know if you are insane or inspired. But I think you're insane."

The next day he texted me: "The jury is still out."

Brother Joe was kidding, but the program was real and quickly gained steam.

If we really believed that addiction is a spiritual disease with devastating psychological and physiological ramifications, then why wasn't the Church systemically providing a spiritual remedy for those who were sick and suffering? Why wasn't the Church out there with an amplified voice saying, "We get it. Come home."? The answer was that members of the Church — lay people and clergy alike — hadn't been trained and ready for addressing the problem of addiction and especially the opioid onslaught.

My next challenge was figuring out how to take what was on two pages of paper and change it into something tangible that could be a gift to the Church. Brother Joe told me to go to Fr. Mike Barth, General Custodian of the Missionary Servants of the Most Holy Trinity.

When I became a member of the recovery retreat ministry, I was given a book of missionary cenacle meditations from the writings of Father Judge. A section from a December 1926 sermon addressed to lay people in Puerto Rico struck me deeply, and it was this that I read to Father Mike when we spoke over the phone:

> We hear frequently of a terrible disaster, many lives are lost. This scourge may have been an earthquake, a hurricane, or indeed any catastrophe. The whole world is shocked; aid is rushed from every quarter to [the] stricken. What do such misfortunes amount to in comparison to the misery and torments of the thousands upon thousands who, unless helped by you, will live

and die without a knowledge or love of God and be lost for all eternity? Do you realize that unless something is done at once, a generation and the children of that generation and their children will be lost to God, lost to Jesus Christ, lost to His religion, lost to heaven and will be lost, indeed for all eternity? That you may realize this appalling situation, lest you be indifferent to it, we have been sent to fasten this obligation on your conscience. You cannot be indifferent. Unless these multitudes are helped by you they will live without a knowledge or love of God and be lost for all eternity. You may answer: "What is that to me? I am trying to save my own soul. Am I my brother's keeper?" You certainly are.[3]

These words fired me up. I read them to anyone I could. The work I was being called to was clearly a contemporary iteration of the work Father Judge had set out to do a century prior. There was no difference between when I was trying to do and what Father Judge called us to do. iTHIRST was one of Father Judge's missions, even if he never saw it in his earthly life. His prophetic vision of the Church playing a role in these great societal maladies stirred me to take it to a different level. I knew we needed to expand it for the whole Church.

It felt gutsy to read Father Mike a quote from his own founder, but he was very open to it. "Listen," I said, "this is what Father Judge is talking about. We have to do something."

Father Mike recommended me to Br. John Skrodinsky, then the Director of Mission. I went to Brother John with the same quote. He, too, listened, and then asked what we could do with it.

I didn't know. I had a plan, but I didn't know what to do with it. Brother Joe advised me to start writing something, but I didn't know where to start. I just had this two-page plan and a page from a book with a quote underlined in pink.

I didn't know, but God did.

How iTHIRST Took Shape

I was teaching voice lessons at the time, and I went to teach a class in my mother-in-law's basement on an electric keyboard. My student's mother was a kind Catholic woman who was always interested in what I was doing outside of teaching.

When I told her about what I was trying to figure out, she told me about a friend of hers who worked for the Archdiocese of Boston. The friend's division was actively figuring out how to enable parishes to become more competent in dealing with people suffering from substance use disorders. They had an Opioid Task Force, and they were looking for resources.

Here's the funny thing: Father Judge was from Boston. Quickly I saw that he was leading us home.

So in 2017, Brother Joe and I went to Boston to attend an Archdiocesan Opioid Task Force meeting, where I presented all I'd fleshed out regarding what I thought the Church needed to do.

Those in attendance were enthusiastic and ready to get started. Except that I still hadn't written anything.

I began writing, and the curriculum came to me in pieces — titles and then sections here and there — all while I prayed for wisdom and guidance. Over the next three years I wrote, while the Opioid Task Force test-piloted the program I was writing. Ultimately, I created almost two hundred pages, despite not knowing where to start.

To test-pilot the program, we needed people. As we developed the training in Boston, one of our greatest proponents was Mother Olga of the Sacred Heart, founder and mother servant of the Daughters of Mary of Nazareth. Mother Olga was working with women in transition, women incarcerated or in halfway houses or shelters. Her sisters tended to those sick and suffering, and she recognized that her sisters needed a greater understanding of the nature of addiction. She brought her sisters, plus many other people from a variety of backgrounds, to my training and helped it to take root.

The next step was to have it academically certified. This process happened through Seton Hall University, due to my having earned my Master of Theology degree there and subsequently maintained connections with various professors and administrators. Seton Hall gave me my theological background (through the Immaculate Conception School of Theology — there's Our Lady again), as well as my joy in learning about my faith. It gave me peers who likewise wanted to give their lives to the Lord, as clergy or as laypeople. So when folks at Seton Hall found out what I was doing, they wanted to promote it. They were proud of the work I was doing, and for their support and academic stamp of approval I was and remain grateful.

Today, time and again, I hear that the best thing about the curriculum is that while it's based in Scripture, it's corroborated by clinical research, such as articles published in *Psychology Today* and books like *Drug Dealer, MD*. To work through the curriculum is to be awakened to the gifts we've already been given through our faith.

The curriculum has quickly enrolled students from outside New Jersey and even from other countries in its virtual capacity. We are everywhere, because that's where the people who need us are — they're everywhere.

Crushing the Stigma

Losing someone to substance use disorder is very different from losing someone to another disease. When addiction is involved, people tend to look at the family of the deceased with a jaundiced eye. There's this perception of "He did it to himself. What did you expect?" Families are embarrassed. Spouses of those who have died because of this affliction are asked, "Did you know they had a problem when you got married?" Parents feel that the death of a child due to substance use disorder is a commentary on their parenting and fear that they will be judged.

When we were test-piloting the program, Mother Olga shared that she was unnerved that parents in her diocese were not giving their children who died of substance use disorder the Rite of Christian Burial. In their grief, these parents didn't feel welcome, comforted, or at home in the Church. She wanted to know: How do we communicate that their loved ones were no less than anyone else?

We need to acknowledge, and then eliminate, the societal stigma that introduces particular challenges to getting help, for both afflicted persons and those who love them. First, those who work with these populations must understand the physiology, psychology, and spirituality of the disease of addiction. To accompany someone out of the abyss of addiction, the ITSC must appreciate the inherent impossibility of intimacy with God, others, and the self within the scope of the attachment.

We cannot escape the challenges and frustrations of ministering to such a particularly vulnerable and marginalized population, but appropriate formation can help potential companions walk the road. This formation means cultivating tremendous compassion and developing pastoral care strategies for navigating the loss that comes from the disease, as well as the stigma related to that loss. People who are addicted may over-intellectualize their situations. They may express disdain for God. Or they may be deeply pious people who simply can't stay clean and sober. ITSCs come face to face with a broad range of situations, but we can learn strategies to employ in this work.

Our role is to be compassionate, meaning "to suffer with." Neel Burton, author of *Heaven and Hell: The Psychology of the Emotions*, writes in *Psychology Today* that compassion "is more engaged than simple empathy and is associated with an active desire to alleviate the suffering of its object. With empathy, I share your emotions; with compassion, I not only share your emotions but also elevate them into a universal and transcending experience."[4] This is a secular way of describing what Pope Francis calls "spiritual accompaniment," which

> must lead others ever closer to God, in whom we attain true freedom. Some people think they are free if they can avoid God; they fail to see that they remain existentially orphaned, helpless, homeless. ... To accompany them would be counterproductive if it became a sort of therapy supporting their self-absorption and ceased to be a pilgrimage with Christ to the Father.[5]

Proper accompaniment therefore helps a soul to "enter on the paths of true growth and awaken a yearning for the Christian ideal: the desire to respond fully to God's love and to bring to fruition what he has sown in our lives."[6]

We're striving to get this ministry to a place where iTHIRST is a household name. We want an ITSC to be able to approach the person in charge of an institution and say, "I'm certified and ready to run this," and then whoever is in charge — priest, chaplain, principal, headmaster, whoever — will be familiar enough with the program to quickly give the green light.

Service Doesn't Require a Degree

While I believe in the program and would love to have as many trained ITSCs as possible, I recognize that not everyone is called to that course of study. Even more foundationally, one doesn't need a degree or certificate to show the sick and suffering compassion. At the start of every course I teach, I tell my students that I already know they all have enough of what they need to serve — before they've opened the manual, before I've spoken a word. Love for God, love for his suffering children, meaningful listening, and the ministry of one's presence really are enough.

Useful as the strategies we teach are, accompanying someone who is addicted or their loved ones doesn't mean having to come up with what love means on one's own. Scripture teaches us where we need to center our hearts. Tradition shows us the life-giving redemptive qualities of serving those whose hearts are heavy as a result of experiencing grief and loss.

Even in my course, I encounter people who think they're not ready or suited for this ministry. They're frightened of the heavy-duty information they're about to take in. But the beauty of the program, what makes it work, is that the ITSCs are working on themselves at the same time. That mutual woundedness is how we take each other's hands on the journey.

It's also what can motivate smaller steps at the parish and diocesan levels as soon as today. We need to bring the disease of addiction out of the darkness into the light in seemingly small but meaningful ways. There are things we can do right now, and we need to recognize our responsibility to do them. Here are some ideas to get you started:

- Start the conversation in your parish. Through education, get the clergy on board, but don't suggest they be responsible for the work. What they can do is mention addicted persons in the prayer of the faithful every day and put a prayer for those with addictions in the bulletin. Encourage your pastor to homilize on relevant topics. Considering that the Twelve Steps are Scripture-based, just about anything can be a relevant topic. There's always a connection. The Bible is full of instances of human beings not being humble, of turning away from God.
- Ask family life and respect life ministries to provide

prayer cards in the vestibule. Offer a monthly Mass intention for those sick and suffering from the disease of addiction and their families, and ask for help in publicizing it so that such persons know where they might find an ear ready to listen.

- Help educate your parish. A simple display case can house pamphlets with local information for Narcotics Anonymous, Alcoholics Anonymous, Al-Anon, and Nar-Anon, including meeting times and locations. Post links to the same on your parish website. Invite fellowship meetings to take place, and then share dates and times on social media.

- Ask your Rosary society to pray monthly for the souls of those lost to addiction, as well as for those struggling and their families.

- Host an event recognizing Overdose Awareness Month in August (perhaps on August 31, which is Overdose Awareness Day) or Recovery Awareness Month in September. These are excellent times to invite a speaker to discuss the spirituality of addiction recovery in your parish, as either a one-night event or an extended retreat. Increase the impact by using this framework to initiate spiritual and corporal works of mercy for those who are afflicted, for their families, and for those who have died.

- Include the youth. Awareness isn't only for adults. I frequently talk to religious education students, often those preparing for confirmation, about the disease of addiction, using age-appropriate language. Young people need to know about the dignity of every human life. All Catholics, young and old, need to see everyone they encounter as a brother or sister in Christ, no matter the circumstance.

How many families do you know with no family members affected by addiction? I can't think of any. This problem is everywhere, which means we need to provide options everywhere. We need to include those dealing with addiction in our parishes, so that they know they have a home in the Church.

The final assignment in the ITSC training asks the student to create a plan for incorporating education and resources at a parish level. Time and again, I am amazed at the creative thinking that flows from realizing and accepting that the Church needs to play a role in remediating this situation and so many other societal maladies.

The Church and the Faith are so relevant to our human struggles. We have forgotten to remind people of that. We need to learn or relearn how to espouse the truth and how to reach out to the vulnerable and marginalized with a sincere offer of spiritual consolation.

It's Not Always a Happy Ending

My friend Melinda was a participant in the pilot stage of the ITSC training in a retreat format at the Shrine of St. Joseph in 2018. She was a professor at Seton Hall and her son, Nunzio, was struggling with heroin addiction. She found the program to be transformative, and she consequently brought me to address her students in a CORE course aptly named "Journey of Transformation." All incoming freshmen and sophomores must take CORE courses, and different professors lend their area of expertise to their approach.

Melinda's students read through excerpts of the personal stories of transformation that come to us from Aristotle, Plato, Saint Thomas Aquinas, Saint Augustine, Dante, persons in the Bhagavad Gita, and more. These writings reveal an explanation of their authentic selves that leads them closer to the God of their understanding. There's no better metaphor for the experience of emerging from the abyss of addiction and onto the road of recovery than "the journey of transformation."

Who would be a great present-day example of a journey of transformation? Someone in recovery.

Within Melinda's course offering was yet another option: to participate in service learning projects throughout the semester. To this end, iTHIRST partnered with Seton Hall's Center for Community Research and Engagement under the auspices of director Timothy Hoffman to shape and form servant leaders.

In "Journey of Transformation," Melinda constructed an amazing course that ties the CORE curriculum into the concept of making this journey as a person in recovery. Take, for example, Plato's Allegory of the Cave. A person is chained to the wall of a cave. He sees these shadows behind him and doesn't know what they are. He thinks it's one thing, but it's something else. When he is unchained, he goes outside and sees something different. Someone afflicted with addiction has the same experience. Once she commences her journey of transformation on the road to recovery, she understands that what she had perceived was not reality.

Melinda and I dubbed the folks who would speak to the class "recovery experts." Some of our "experts" are in long-term recovery, others short-term. All of them desire to share their experience, strength, and hope with students.

At the end of Melinda's CORE semester, students must write a paper on their service learning experience with iTHIRST. So many have shared that they had a loved one who suffered, that now they understand what that person was going through, and that they've developed greater compassion. Some students admit they are in recovery themselves. Some admit they have a problem. Some confess that we've helped them dispel the myth of the "other." These moments make it so clear that addiction is not a problem that affects only a few or only this sort of person or only someone who's had that sort of experience. Furthermore, this program is how we create disciples who will go out and work on the margins, and I hope it's an approach that other universities will begin to mimic.

And what about Melinda and her son? The first recovery expert spoke in Melinda's CORE classroom on September 20, 2018. Two days later, her son overdosed and died.

She told me that she would not have been able to emerge from her grief if she hadn't had iTHIRST accompanying her. The pain she endured was unbearable, even with that support.

Today, Nunzio's life on earth is over, but his legacy continues in his mother. She is a warrior fixed on raising the eyes of the faithful to see we all have a role to play. She does it in her work at Seton Hall, in her community, and in the other ways she honors his life on earth. Outside of the university, she is an ITSC, working with those afflicted and their loved ones in her parish community and now in neighboring churches that yet don't have someone trained.

Melinda's work is helping to crush the stigma and encouraging Catholics, young and old alike, to understand our responsibility as Catholic Christians. We are all responsible to help those on the periphery. I return to that quote from Father Judge: "You may answer: 'What is that to me? I am trying to save my own soul. Am I my brother's keeper?' You certainly are."

Reflect

- The Holy Spirit infused Fr. Thomas Judge, founder of the Missionary Servants of the Most Holy Trinity, with a profound missionary zeal and a deep desire to serve those who are poor and abandoned, those who reside in the "tangled parts of the Vineyard of Christ."[7] In what ways has the Holy Spirit inspired you in your life? How do you remain open to listening to the promptings of the Spirit?

- Stigma surrounds all sorts of addictions, but particularly substance use disorders. Have you ever felt stigmatized for any reason? What impact did it have on your spiritual, emotional, or mental well-being?
- By beginning the conversation in our parishes, we Catholics have the opportunity to bring the subject of addiction out of the darkness and into the light. Revisit the ways our parishes can become proactive on pages 73–74. What are some other ideas you can bring to your parish to welcome home those who have been underserved for so long?

Pray

O God, my Heavenly Creator, imbue me with the missionary zeal of Father Judge, that I may not fear the thorns of the "tangled parts of the Vineyard," but rather embrace them in humility.

Grant that my ears will be ever attentive to the needs of my brothers and sisters and always open to sharing in their heartaches and their hopes.

Grant that my eyes will always see the face of the suffering Christ in those I serve, no matter their circumstances or attitude.

Grant that my heart will always be filled with your love and compassion and a desire to serve those who are most vulnerable and marginalized.

Grant that my soul will magnify you, just as Mary's did, for no human person has ever offered themselves so fully in self-gift as she, the Mother of God.

I ask all of this in the name of Jesus Christ, our Lord and Savior.

Amen.

5

It's Going to Hurt

Being a recovering addict, I've experienced many years of extreme and crippling emotional pain. My own thoughts led me to believe that being numb was better than feeling anything at all. Truth is, numbing it for so long only made it worse when I finally felt it.

The pain of feeling defeated as a mother and losing my babies was the most excruciating pain my heart ever felt. I literally lost myself and any part of identity I ever had. I was mentally and emotionally bankrupt. My body was in a state of shock and everything felt as if it was just shutting down and crumbling. At that point I was in fight-or-flight mode. Every fiber of my being wanted to fight and become sober for my children. Sadly, my disease chose flight mode and put my children and family through many years of their own pain based on my poor decisions.

It wasn't until several years later that I had a very profound spiritual experience and realized the cure for pain was actually in the pain itself. I had a mustard seed of faith at this time because after overdosing, being on my deathbed with a heart and lung infection, you couldn't tell me there wasn't some type of greater entity. That grew over time and I realized my pain and suffering could be made purposeful.

I heard that in order to manifest a purpose, there has to be some level of passion, and you cannot have passion without some level of suffering. For the next few years and presently I embrace my pain so that it can produce glory.

Being a child of God, I realize my exact purpose. I hold on to my passion for helping those in need, and currently I get to work with others on a daily basis to enlighten, empower, and encourage them on their painful journeys through the same process.

— Sara

Contemporary culture features a lot of misconceptions and false understandings, and one of the most damaging is the ideal — or better, the idol — of not experiencing pain. We want things to be easy, quick, gratifying. No one should have to suffer, the narrative tells us. It's uncomfortable. No, thank you. You only live once, you know.

Lembke explains that until very recently in human history, "we have understood pain in our lives to serve at least two useful functions": as both a warning system and an opportunity for spiritual growth.[1] This understanding is no longer *en vogue*. Rather, she writes:

Modern American culture regards pain as anathema, to

be avoided at all cost. This new way of looking at pain arises from the belief that pain can cause permanent neurological damage that lays the foundation for future pain. This new conception holds true for both mental and physical pain, and it has been a major contributor to the prescription drug epidemic.[2]

Our culture tempts and teases us with the false idol of a pain-free life, neglecting the reality that if we are to be formed in Christ — if we are to be conformed to Christ — we are necessarily going to suffer. To worship Jesus doesn't just mean to sing praise and worship, write a check to the food pantry, and keep on with the bubbles we've constructed for ourselves. Being a true disciple of Christ means living in the tension of a great dichotomy of joy and suffering. The apostle Peter writes that while "now for a little while you may have to suffer various trials," at the same time, the follower of Christ is able to "rejoice with unutterable and exalted joy. As the outcome of your faith you obtain the salvation of your souls" (1 Pt 1:6, 8–9).

When we bring our pain to Jesus, he redeems it. He makes something beautiful out of what is broken in us. Our society has lost that concept. It sees no value in suffering, so it eschews any kind of pain — physical, emotional, or spiritual.

Jesus never promised that sharing his Good News was going to be easy. In fact, he told us it was going to be hard, really hard, even crushing at times. In each of the Gospels, Jesus tells his disciples that they — that we — must deny ourselves, take up our crosses, and follow him (see Mt 16:24; Mk 8:34; Lk 14:27; Jn 12:26). There is going to be pain. There is going to be death. But, as Catholics, we know there is also eternal life, to which we are all called to strive.

Walking with people on their own roads to God is difficult. We who are called to be companions face big challenges, because

specific challenges face vulnerable and marginalized populations who are traditionally underserved or underheard. But life
with Christ requires so much more than consolation and comfort. We necessarily have to suffer. No one suffered more than
Christ, who gave himself knowing that not everyone was going
to accept his love for them.

Many of the faithful are familiar with the spiritual excellence
of the Desert Fathers, those early hermits who lived an ascet-
ic life in Egypt. Fewer know much about the Desert Mothers,
though writings of three of these women are included in the
Apophthegmata Patrum, or *Sayings of the Desert Fathers.* Amma
Syncletica was one of these — "amma" means "mother," and her
name, Syncletica, means "assembly," so she was "Mama Assembly" — and many followed her for her spiritual direction. These
are her words:

> There is labor and great struggle for the impious who
> are converted to God, but after that comes inexpressible
> joy. A man who wants to light a fire first is plagued by
> smoke, and the smoke drives him to tears, yet finally he
> gets the fire he wants. So also it is written: Our God is a
> consuming fire. Hence we ought to light the divine fire
> in ourselves with labor and with tears.[3]

To put it in twenty-first century terms, Amma Synclectica
"gets me."

Scripture tells us, "And after you have suffered a little while, the
God of all grace, who has called you to his eternal glory in Christ,
will himself restore, establish, and strengthen you" (1 Pt 5:10).
There is an obvious dichotomy between these two feelings, between inexpressible joy and the sadness of suffering. Life without
loss, without struggle, isn't a possibility in this fallen world.

We could mourn, grieve, and lament that. Or we could see in

it a path forward, toward eternal life.

I go back to the parable of the Good Samaritan, particularly to the priest and Levite who are fearful of losing their holiness should they invite any degree of intimacy with the bloody and broken man before them. Jesus clearly teaches that these two achieve the very opposite of their aim. To the scholar of the law, to whom he addresses the parable, he gives the Two Great Commandments to follow to gain eternal life: "You shall love the Lord your God with all your heart, and with all your soul, and with all your strength, and with all your mind; and your neighbor as yourself" (Lk 10:27). This mission is hurtful, *and* we are called to give it our all. We can't let that same kind of fear hold us back.

Fasten This Obligation to Your Conscience

A few years back, I told my husband someone that I worked with had passed away. I said, "I can't believe it."

He asked what I couldn't believe. This is my work, he reminded me. This pain is part of the mission.

"Fasten this obligation to your conscience," Father Judge wrote. Today, my copy of the book in which I read that naturally flips open to this page, since I've referred to it so many times. As Christians, we cannot be concerned only with our own souls. Saint Paul wrote to the Corinthians, "I will most gladly spend and be spent for your souls" (2 Cor 12:15). Likewise, Saint Teresa Benedicta of the Cross counsels, "We do not love a person because he does good. His value is not that he does good, even if he perhaps come to light for this reason. Rather, he himself is valuable and we love him for his own sake." The spiritual life of our brothers and sisters is the most important thing we could care about. We need to believe this. We need to tell this to our brothers and sisters who, frankly, have never heard it before.

This mission is about more than addiction. It's about bringing souls home to Christ.

Let's be real. No one wants to be estranged from his family. No one wants to wake up dopesick or hungover. We can't write off our brothers and sisters, thinking that if they cause destruction and die it's their own issue. We need to ask what has brought people into such a frightening, miserable, scary, messy situation, what has turned it into a tortured compulsion — and then show compassion.

I didn't make that up. If you're listening to the Gospel message, it's very simple. There's never a "them" and an "us." Jesus says, "A new commandment I give to you, that you love one another; even as I have loved you, that you also love one another. By this all men will know that you are my disciples, if you have love for one another" (Jn 13:34–35). I won't pretend it's easy, but I am convinced it is simple, because of the unending and ever-new mercy of God.

In Deuteronomy, Moses warns against provoking the Lord to anger by "[acting] corruptly by making a graven image in the form of anything" (4:25). "The Lord will scatter you among the peoples," Moses tells them, but that will not be the end of the story (4:27). There is hope. There is always hope:

> But from there you will seek the LORD your God, and you will find him, if you search after him with all your heart and with all your soul. When you are in tribulation, and all these things come upon you in the latter days, you will return to the LORD your God and obey his voice, for the LORD your God is a merciful God; he will not fail you or destroy you or forget the covenant with your fathers which he swore to them. (4:29–31)

Scripturally, we can draw a clear line from Moses' teaching to the parable of the prodigal son, who abandoned his father. In time, the son in the parable admits his faults to himself, to God, and then to his father, to whom he returns with a contrite heart. The prodigal son reminds us of the mercy of our loving Father, who is always ready to welcome us home.

All throughout Sacred Scripture, God tells us that he knows we're going to worship false idols, but if we return to him with a repentant heart, he will take us home. Over and over, he tells us that he wants us home with him. And so it remains today. When we turn to the Father in love, he welcomes us home. To me, that is the utmost in hope. Yes, it means we have to do the work in ourselves. We have to recognize our faults and failures; we must have the desire to go home. But there remains this beautiful promise that he is waiting for us. There is always that guarantee of mercy. We turn away from it, but the guarantee never goes away.

James and the Golden Scar

The Japanese technique *kintsugi* ("golden seams"), or *kintsukuroi* ("golden repair"), is the art of visibly repairing broken pottery with lacquer and gold pigment. Imperfections are not hidden but rather highlighted. Pieces created with this technique have a unique and powerful beauty — one possible only because of the previous damage done to them.

I came across this technique in a meditation on Scripture, specifically Saint Paul discussing the thorn in his flesh, which he asks the Lord to take away (see 2 Cor 12:7). The Lord replies, "My grace is sufficient for you, for my power is made perfect in weakness," to which Saint Paul responds, "I will all the more gladly boast of my weaknesses, that the power of Christ may rest upon me" (2 Cor 12:9). The reflection I read drew the comparison between kintsugi and Saint Paul's affliction, explaining that "the broken and weak places in our lives can become places where God's power and glory may shine. He holds us together, transforms us, and makes our weaknesses beautiful."[4] To witness somebody emerge from the abyss and begin to live a life of abundance and in service is the greatest gift to the companion. It is kintsugi manifest.

Let me tell you about my best friend, James. James is the only person I talk to multiple times a day besides my husband. When I met James on retreat at Trinity House, he was in very early recovery. That weekend was the first time that he had considered what it means to have a spiritual life. He'd never thought about it before. He was angry at God and angry at the evil one. He knew he was brought into recovery for a reason.

I've worked with him for over six years, and I've watched him evolve as a speaker telling his story. He's no longer living on benches in Newark Penn Station or under trees. Now I call him a colleague and know that I can call upon him to reach out to young people.

James motivates me every day. In every person I work with, I see James. His story is all the more beautiful and impactful because of his scars. It wouldn't have been that way — it couldn't have been that way — if he hadn't endured that suffering.

Witnessing Resurrection

When a loved one says, "It's me or the dope," the answer seems obvious. Of course the right choice is the relationship, the person, the love. But the physiological attachment the brain forms, along with the fear of dealing with the collateral damage in one's life, can make that choice feel heavy, unbearable, impossible. Yet I've seen people emerge from that pain. I've watched people step out of the abyss of addiction to find meaning and purpose, even as they carry their crosses.

I don't use that phrase, "carry their crosses," lightly. Early recovery, in particular, really is like carrying the cross. There are stumbling blocks and choppy waters and still a great deal of suffering. This is to be expected. Pope St. John Paul II wrote in *Salvifici Doloris* that "the *Redemption* was accomplished *through the*

Cross of Christ, that is, *through his suffering.* ... In whatever form, suffering seems to be, and is, almost *inseparable from man's earthly existence.*"[5] That can sound dire and desolate, if you don't know the end of the story: Through Christ's suffering on the cross, *"human suffering itself has been redeemed."*[6]

When people begin to find their own resurrection, they become images of that inexpressible joy. To watch someone who previously came off as reprehensible be transformed into a person who acknowledges and honors his own unique dignity is to witness resurrection.

The secular world agrees that suffering can be transformative. In the field of psychology, this idea is called posttraumatic growth. Studies on this subject corroborate what we already know: Individuals who endure a period of suffering often emerge with new skills; greater inner strength, confidence, compassion, and appreciation of the little things in life; more intimate relationships; and deeper spiritual awareness.[7] This doesn't mean we should seek out suffering. But when it is part of our lives, we need to acknowledge that to deny the pain we experience is to miss opportunities to develop resilience and push our limits.

The lens of Catholic spirituality also teaches that the one who suffers is not the only one who is changed. When we sit and talk to somebody who's suffered and we share in their suffering, we become one another, to put it in the terms of Marcia Wakeland. Wakeland is co-founder of The Listening Post, a place designed for confidential listening in Anchorage, Alaska. She describes this mode of connection between people as a nest: "We were both there. There was no separation. I cannot think of a more important piece of spiritual knowledge than this. It makes me feel not homeless; the relationship has created a nest that holds us."[8]

When we sit with another, we gain so much. Even if our experiences haven't been the same, we've all felt broken, lonely, resentful, and angry at God. If we're intellectually honest, we can admit to those feelings; we can be vulnerable enough to enter into someone else's experience and invite them into ours. In that way, their resurrection becomes our new life, too.

Acknowledging the Challenges

On the road to recovery lies pain — not only pain for the individuals suffering and their families, but also the challenges specific to this particular accompaniment for those of us who walk with them.

In the past, addiction in families was dealt with in a tough-love manner, which often meant physically cutting the person off and rarely did any real good. Today, a more common approach involves loving that person unconditionally, but setting appropriate boundaries. Those boundaries make way for the self-emptying, or *kenosis*, that is the foundation of Twelve Step programs. The steps are, at their root, a Scripture-based process of peeling back the layers we all carry in order to find our authentic selves. It's good for all of us, no matter how close we are to the disease of addiction, to determine how we can more deeply connect with who we are, so that we can strive each day for a closer relationship with God.

Individuals and family members living with or alongside addiction tend to compromise in their relationships, diminish themselves and their own needs, and under- or overcompensate, all as a means of maintaining some sense of stability. These boundary issues can become a challenge in a relationship with an ITSC.

Often as ITSCs we encounter stagnation issues, in which the person we walk with doesn't seem to be making any spiritual progress. Here, we can take encouragement from Saint John of the Cross: "Do not say, 'Oh, the soul is making no progress because it isn't doing anything,' for I will prove to you that the soul is doing a great deal by doing nothing.'" Often a lot is going on under the surface, and the blessing of presence is gift enough. We can also see this as an opportunity for us as a companion, as well as the one afflicted, to grow in patience and trust in the Lord. Sr. Faustina Maria Pia, SV, author of the Litany of Trust, writes:

> God will never ask us to give more than we have. Although the task He invites us to may exceed our capacities, the gift of our love and consent to Him is all He is looking for. In fact, because things don't seem to add up in our estimation, the gift of our trust in His power pleases Him greatly. Our trust in Him gives Him the freedom to multiply our small efforts, allowing God to pour His love through us. [9]

This advice is similarly relevant when we, as companions, find ourselves struggling with "fix-it" frustration: when we want so badly to make things right for the individual we are ministering to, sometimes to the point of pain. The reality is that there's nothing we can do to bring someone out of that abyss if she doesn't want to move. The mother of a young woman addicted to heroin described to me her feeling of helplessness as being like "sitting on a boat with a life preserver, watching her drown."

This tension can be overwhelming for companions when not properly attended to. But still, this is the nature of this work. This is the suffering we are called to share in, and it takes courage to do that. Wakeland writes:

> It takes courage to listen to stories that appear to have no way of redemption or reconciliation. It requires dedication to listen to the same story over and over, while watching an addict worsen before our eyes, wondering if he too will freeze this winter while drinking or taking Spice, heroin, or meth. It is a brave thing to care for other human beings, knowing that this may help them more

than anything else you have to offer — and then to let them go.[10]

To date, I've lost 63 people whom I have spent time directly with, spoken with, worked with, been on retreat with. We don't save everyone. There is still such darkness and such pain. But I carry on with faith and with hope. I know there is a light in the darkness, and the darkness has not — cannot, will not — overcome it (see Jn 1:5).

Saving, But Not Savior

I have an extensive collection of bracelets in my home shrine. I used to wear these bracelets, given to me by people on retreats where I'd spoken. At the end of these events, people would go down to the gift shop at the center, buy me a bracelet, and ask me to wear it to remember them and to pray for them. And I did. I wore them. I prayed.

In 2018, I was in a car accident, and I needed years of physical therapy for terrible ongoing back spasms as a result. One day I worked with a new physical therapist, who noted the correlation between the emotional weight of the bracelets I wore and my continued spasms. I was carrying too much physically, and I was carrying too much emotionally.

He encouraged me to symbolically let them go: to think of each person as I took the appropriate bracelet off and not to discard them, but rather find the proper place for them. I needed to draw a line as to how much I could give, both for myself and for those I was trying to serve. Once I learned this anew during confession with a visiting priest. "There is one Savior of the world, and it ain't you," he told me.

I followed the physical therapist's recommendation, and I have not had a spasm since. My bracelets still sit in my prayer space, and I still pray for each of those people, but I do so now within healthier boundaries.

Today, I only wear one bracelet, depicting the Blessed Mother. I can carry only so much for my birds, those I accompany, and I can entrust the rest to her. My mission does not call me to deplete myself. My mission calls me to invite suffering people out of the darkness and into the light, so they can listen to the promptings of the Holy Spirit and live in the hope that my Savior and theirs will do the rest.

I marvel at how different I am now from when I first worked with John. Then, I was convinced that he would do well because I came into the equation, to love him and feed him and find him and share God's love with him and bring him places. Now I have a much greater understanding of what is asked of me, and absolute acceptance of my limitations in serving others. This is freeing. This is what allows me to continue.

If you believe you bear the weight of someone's life or death, it overwhelms you. Of course it does; that's so much more than God asks of us. No, we are to shepherd people to the Shepherd. Through our love, caring, and concern, we invite our brothers and sisters to see God's ineffable love and mercy, to know that God is ready and waiting for them.

At that point, determining what happens next is in his hands and in each person's human intention.

Reflect

- We live in a society that eschews pain, whether it be physical, emotional, mental, or spiritual. Yet we know that so often, from and through our pain and suffering, we emerge more compassionate toward and understanding of others as we conform ourselves to Christ. How has pain or suffering been spiritually transformative in your life?
- Amma Syncletica understood that all those advanc-

ing toward God would undergo great toil, but soon after they would experience inexpressible joy. What challenges have you faced in your personal journey of transformation, as you have sought a deeper intimacy with God?

- Throughout Sacred Scripture, God constantly reminds us that when we develop a contrite heart, he in his ineffable mercy will always welcome us home, like the loving father in the parable of the prodigal son. At different times, we have probably acted like each of the three characters in this story. When have you welcomed someone home in love and mercy as the Father did? When have you felt the mercy of another, like the prodigal son? When, like the older brother, have you glanced in resentment at someone you deemed undeserving of forgiveness?

Pray

Dear Father of Divine Mercy, today I offer you all my pain and all my suffering, that I may draw closer to you and your wounds.

Help me to understand that my suffering and sorrow are a great gift that allows me to have the compassion to understand and accompany others as they struggle.

Even though I will encounter challenges in ministering to those on the peripheries, may I be heartened to remember that there will soon be inexpressible joy, just as Amma Syncletica understood.

May I always seek to welcome home the prodigal children in my life, with love, with mercy, and with compassion, as you did, O Lord.

Amen.

❧

6

Broken Families and
Mother Church

*When I was in my first weeks of sobriety, I sought out
guidance from the people in my church that I trusted. I
was taught simple prayers and invited to attend some retreats. Those resources were a lifesaver in my early months
and continued to be a source of support for years.*

*There are almost twenty-one million Americans with
at least one addiction to a substance and only ten percent receive treatment.[1] Globally, the number of alcoholics alone grows to nearly three hundred million people.[2]
These numbers should be of grave interest to the Church,
as they dwarf nearly every other common pastoral or
ministerial concern.*

This is a condition that devastates families as well

*as individuals. One could assert that the Church has an
obligation to remain relevant in the twenty-first century,
and with the proper focus of education, commitment, and
resources, united ecclesial efforts have an unparalleled opportunity to make a difference here.*

*Pastorally speaking, it would be prudent to recognize
the need for massive ministerial action as a direct response
to the Gospel. Personally speaking, I wouldn't have been
able to stay sober had I not had support from my parish.*
— Blitch

I had been offering non-denominational spirituality sessions
at a Christian community-based residential treatment facility for about a year when I got into a conversation with one of
the residents. He was a fellow in his forties who had been there
for some time. He was always appreciative of my sharing and
singing and my efforts to get the individuals there to develop
an intimacy with the God of their understanding. This was the
first time that he engaged me in conversation after the weekly
session. After he shared that he had been in active addiction for
decades, I decided to dig in more deeply with him.

"You're here now. Are you ready this time?" I said.

"Yes," he replied.

When I asked what the change was for him, he told me that
for many years, he would call his mother, and she would always
answer the phone. She would say, "I love you. Are you ready to
make a change?" When he was reticent or didn't respond, she'd
say, "Call me when you are" and gently hang up. This went on for
years. Finally he realized what he was doing to his own mother,
and that was the day he came into recovery.

Even in damaged and dysfunctional relationships, our families have a powerful hold on us, for better or for worse. For this

man in the throes of addiction, the tenacity of his mother's love was the motivation he needed to start walking the road to recovery. For loved ones, the pain of negotiating the collateral damage of their family member's affliction creates a ripple effect that affects every part of their lives and even beyond themselves. The idea that "I'm not hurting anyone else but myself" is absolutely not true. Addiction affects individuals, their families, their communities (which miss out on the blessings and contributions of those who isolate themselves), as well as workplaces and governments (which suffer reduced productivity). This is yet another reason why addiction — and substance use disorder in particular — is everybody's problem.

Fighting for Families

For our purposes of amplifying the voice of the Church in substance use disorder recovery, let's focus on the family members of those afflicted. According to the National Center for Drug Abuse Statistics, 31.9 million Americans aged twelve years and older currently use illegal drugs.[3] This means their families easily number in the millions as well. These are people we see at the grocery store, people who sit next to us in the pews, people who are aching each and every day, often unseen.

One person's addiction upends the whole family unit. Family members tend to take on their own, often destructive, behaviors as they desperately seek to protect or save their loved ones. Individuals erase boundaries between themselves and their loved ones, thus developing patterns of giving more than is appropriate in other relationships. Or they gradually drift from their communities because they are embarrassed by their family life; they ultimately find themselves isolated, while inadvertently perpetuating the troubling behavior of their loved one.

I witnessed a situation in which a mother suffering from alcoholism was unable to participate in the lives of her children.

The eldest child stepped up and started parenting the family out of necessity. This kid no longer participated in the community as a young person; he wasn't doing the social things his peers were. He was desperate to protect his younger siblings from the effects of their mother's drinking as well as protect his mother from the consequences of her alcoholism.

In many ways, he was enabling her behavior in an attempt to find stability and balance in the home. Dr. Patrick Carnes, founder of the International Institute for Trauma and Addiction Professionals, describes enabling behavior as "[concentrating] on meeting the needs of another person and [taking] responsibility for that person's behavior. No boundaries exist and consequently no privacy exists. Again, a pattern of living in the extreme emerges."[4] These patterns, especially when left unaddressed, not only are extremely difficult to break, but also make it increasingly difficult for family members to seek help.

It can be difficult to see, even for those involved, but parents, siblings, and children of those addicted to drugs and alcohol often experience shame, guilt, and feelings of unworthiness and abandonment that parallel the feelings of the one afflicted. For the most part, families tend to see the addiction through the prism of their own suffering, and they can't conceive of the pain the afflicted person is feeling. In the same vein, the afflicted person typically struggles to recognize the pain his addiction is causing the people he loves. People on both sides of these relationships don't realize the other side is in pain. That ignorance keeps all involved out of the treatment, help, and fellowship that could lead family members, too, to a renewed life of abundance.

As much as we need to crush the societal stigma surrounding addiction for those who are suffering, we also need to eliminate it for their families. Those suffering from substance use disorder are frequently ostracized from society for their behaviors. Family members are ostracized by association, though sometimes this separation from others is self-inflicted. They can be so ashamed that they don't bother reaching out to recovery, loss, or bereavement groups.

Take a less charged example. When someone dies of lung cancer, what's normally the first question that comes to mind: Did he smoke? If the answer is yes, even if it's not explicit, many people can offer only mitigated sympathy. The death is a loss — but under the surface lurks a sense that his illness was, to some degree, of his own choosing.

It's the same with addiction. The popularly accepted conviction that those who are slaves to drugs or alcohol choose their fate means that when someone loses his life to substance use, family members fear others will look at them as if to say, "Your loved one chose this demise." Parents fear that their child's death by overdose will be seen as a negative reflection of their parenting.

In chapter 4, I mentioned Mother Olga and her concern that parents were not giving their children the Rite of Christian Burial when their death was attributable to addiction. Theirs is a compounded tragedy, for the deceased as well as for those who remain. This last, but certainly not least, of the corporal works of mercy is being neglected, and the neglect causes great harm. People really believe that God is angry at the one who passed, so they are too embarrassed to have a Christian ceremony. This avoidance should not go on for another second. Christian burial is a clear and all-too-frequently missed opportunity to welcome people back to Mother Church. In those moments of heart-rending pain, those suffering need the comfort of the Eucharist, worship, prayer, and the sacraments.

A Mother's Love

Family dynamics when addiction is involved are like a boat rocked on the seas. The boat is the family, tossed about by the tides of the addiction. They have a space, a need, for someone outside the situation to create a gentle bridge to initiate healing and bring people back to each other. To regain stability and normalcy — or get it for the first time — we, as the Church, need to tend to the broken souls of family and friends of those afflicted: hearing them, seeing them, guiding them back to the all-encompassing love of the Savior.

Imagine you're a parent who has tended to every boo-boo throughout your child's grade school years. You brought forgotten lunches to school. You supported your child's pursuits of sports, theater, and more. Now your child is doing something that's spiraling out of control — and you can't fix it. This reality is devastating.

Imagine you've taken a sacred matrimonial vow to love and support your spouse in sickness and in health. You've been there for each other in times of crisis before, but now your loved one is experiencing something catastrophic, not only to his or her physical being, but to the marriage itself. How do you live that vow out now?

Imagine you have been raised in the shadow of your parent's disease. Now, as an adult, how do you process your grief and resentment from a stolen childhood? How does that affect the family that you may be raising now?

People — parents and children, spouses and friends — need help to hand their loved ones over to God. They need support to remain present for people they love who are struggling with addiction but are not ready for recovery. They need guidance in setting good, healthy boundaries for themselves and their loved ones.

We've already explored the importance of active listening. We must be very gentle with the family members of those afflicted. They're already beating themselves up. In my experience, most respond well to expressions of empathy that help them trust. We can help them to accept the parts of the situation that are out of their control, because only in this act of surrender can they find peace. Unfounded expectations for their loved ones can set them up for further disappointment, whereas showing compassion and reminding them of God's ineffable love and incalculable mercy can be a balm for their fractured spirits.

Family members also often need to know why their loved ones can't "just stop." They need to understand the psychology and physiology of their loved one's hijacked brain. They need to appreciate that the person is operating under extreme duress, and they need coaching to separate the behavior from the individual. Whether the reprehensible behavior is being caused by an iatrogenic force (that is, a legitimately prescribed addictive substance) or by the afflicted person's desire to fill a hole in their soul, none of this diminishes the unique human dignity of the individual. A person's choices do not equal that person.

In his letter to the Ephesians, Saint Paul encourages his listeners to "Put off the old man that belongs to your former manner of life and is corrupt through deceitful lusts, and be renewed in the spirit of your minds, and put on the new man, created after the likeness of God in true righteousness and holiness" (Eph 4:22–24). We always have an opportunity to change, to be converted, to remove one "man," in Saint Paul's language, as we get closer to Christ, and then choose to take on the "new man."

We can take the love of Our Lady, Our Mother, the first disciple of Christ, as the prime example of how to live Christian love. She is "the maximum expression and at the same time the most faithful reflection of what it means to be a new creation in Christ and what the dignity of man redeemed by Christ involves," writes Fr. Juan Luis Bastero, Doctor of Theology and Emeritus Professor of Mariology at the Higher Institute of Religious Sciences of the University of Navarra.[5] Mary, the true mother of us all, is likewise the greatest expression of our Holy and Apostolic Church. Father Bastero writes that "Mary's co-operation in the Christ event and the place she occupies in salvation history help to discover not only the truth about Christ, but also the true face of the Church and the precise nature of man's salvation. … In her is made manifest the change which takes place in man redeemed by Christ."[6]

Mary has walked closely with me throughout my journey ministering to those afflicted and their families. In a profound way, and in more instances than I can fit in these pages, I have experienced her maternal love for me and for those I tend to. I keep an image of Our Lady just over my shoulder when I work or teach classes, to remind me that she is always watching over me, seeing everything I do. I saw Our Mother's love with the development of iTHIRST, and I've seen it in so many other ways throughout the work I do.

When I am close to Mary, I know I can't go wrong; she won't let me.

Mama Mary and Mother Church

Few contemporary conversion stories are more dramatic than that of Fr. Donald Calloway, MIC. Many know Father Calloway as the author of *No Turning Back: A Witness to Mercy*, *Purest of All Lilies: The Virgin Mary in the Spirituality of St. Faustina*, and *Consecration to St. Joseph: The Wonders of Our Spiritual Father*. But before Father Calloway was a Catholic priest and a member of the Congregation of Marian Fathers of the Immaculate Conception, he was addicted to various drugs as well as alcohol, and he lived a promiscuous and criminal lifestyle that, at one point, got him deported from Japan. His conversion took place one night when, feeling depressed, he scanned his parents' bookshelves for a *National Geographic* magazine, to look at the pictures.[7] His parents had recently converted to Catholicism, and what he found instead was a book called *The Queen of Peace Visits Medjugorje* by Joseph Albert Pelletier.

The book initiated a mystical experience that changed his life. "It wasn't long before I realized this book was presenting me an offer to change my life and surrender to something greater than myself — to believe in God and be different," he writes in *No Turning Back*. "It was a revelation that required a revolution in my thinking. Could this be the way out I was looking for?"[8] He describes how he heard Mary rejoicing over his coming to accept the mercy of her Son. "I was so at peace that I felt like a little boy snuggled close to his mother's breast. I was so at peace, so loved, and so at rest that I went into a deep sleep. I hadn't slept like that since I was a young boy."[9]

Not everyone who experiences a conversion can expect to have as tangible an experience as Father Calloway did; but the presence of Mary in his story speaks to Our Lady's desire to be close to her children and to always point us all back to her son, Jesus Christ. Consider Mary's words at the Wedding at Cana: "Do whatever he tells you" (Jn 2:5). What did her son tell us? To love one another as he loved us (see Jn 13:34). That love ought to be unconditional. It needs to go to dark places. It needs to be willing to get messy. It needs to be patient, kind, and forgiving.

In an iTHIRST support group for the friends and families of those suffering from addiction, I witnessed this love extending to Stella,[10] a very devout Catholic woman at the Shrine of St. Joseph. Stella's son had been molested by a family member while Stella was working a night shift. She thought she was doing the right thing by working to support her family and leaving her children in the care of someone she could trust. That son came to suffer from alcoholism. He lost a host of opportunities, jobs, his marriage, and custody of his children. He was living with a tremendous amount of anger and blame.

At the same time, Stella blamed herself. After a while there was no relationship between mother and son, despite how desperate she was for connection to him. Their family dynamic was utterly skewered. It was a whole hot mess of dysfunction.

Stella began coming regularly to the support group meetings, and together we reached out to her son. He is in recovery now, but at that point, he still had a ways to go on his journey of transformation. The more immediate blessing for his mother was developing coping mechanisms to support healthy boundaries and detachment from the situation. Stella was able to find spiritual consolation through her work with the iTHIRST team. The trauma and guilt that she felt, the blame that she put on herself, began to give way to healing. She couldn't let go on her own. But with someone to accompany her, to walk the road by her side, she made progress toward the restoration of her family.

Though a mother herself, Stella needed someone to love her with a mother's love. In this case, iTHIRST made that love manifest for her. This mission, healing the broken, is something we are all called to carry out, as members of Holy Mother Church.

Reflect

- Addiction affects every member of a family, as boundaries fade and individuals become desperate to save their loved one from destructive behaviors. Have you ever powerlessly watched the decline and perhaps demise of a loved one due to circumstances beyond your control?

- Feelings of anger, shame, resentment, isolation, and societal stigma often keep both those who are afflicted and their family members from receiving the appropriate support and treatment. Have you ever been ashamed to ask for help for something?

- Jesus' fervent commandment "to love one another" is bolstered by Our Lady's words at the wedding feast at Cana: "Do whatever he tells you." To follow their words requires radical, self-giving love. How do Mary's words resonate with you in your life? How are you poised to show that love to those around you?

Pray

Holy and loving Father, bless all those who struggle in silence because of the addiction of a loved one.

Remove the shame, guilt, and societal stigma from their hearts, so that they may feel your healing presence in their lives as they seek the help and support of others.

Help them to overcome their fears as they learn to give their loved ones over to you and your will in complete trust.

Let them feel the tender mercy of our Blessed Mother, who, as the greatest expression of our Holy and Apostolic Church, is the true mother of us all.

We ask this in the name of our Savior, Christ Jesus.

Amen.

ᴥ

7

Every Catholic an Apostle

The founder of the Missionary Servants of the Most Holy Trinity, Fr. Thomas Judge, CM, ST, passed on to us the core of his belief: that every Catholic is an Apostle. He further instructed us to live this out in the providence of our everyday lives. There is no more pressing need in our day than the needs of those suffering from addiction.

We Missionary Servants have believed this, following Father Judge's lead, since the 1920s, as he opened Saint Joseph Villa in New Jersey, until the present day in our robust sponsorship of the iTHIRST Initiative. We all have the responsibility, summoned by our baptism, to respond to the scourge of addiction, to educate and equip ourselves, to respond and serve. Addiction is everywhere. We too need to be everywhere in our efforts to respond, embrace those suffering, and offer a path to healing and wholeness.

— Fr. Mike Barth

The Missionary Servants of the Most Holy Trinity — the religious congregation of priests and brothers of which iTHIRST is a mission — was formed in 1921 by Father Judge, a Vincentian priest whose charism was to preserve the Faith, especially among those who were poor and abandoned. As chapter 1 explains, Father Judge prophetically understood that amongst those who are "poor and abandoned" are those suffering from addictions. So his community, known as STs, has long worked with those suffering from various addictions, primarily to alcohol. Before Alcoholics Anonymous existed, Saint Joseph Villa offered a refuge for priests and brothers struggling with alcohol use, "to rehabilitate them for eventual return to active ministry." In fact, it was "the first such residence of its kind in the United States," writes Carl J. Ganz, historian of the Shrine of St. Joseph.[1] The first residents came from the Diocese of Newark, but soon "priests were arriving from Albany, Brooklyn, Long Island, and as far away as Seattle."[2] Within its first fifty years of operation, "the St. Joseph's rehabilitation program had treated priests from Canada, Europe, and South America."[3] The breadth of the program was due, in part, to there being "only six other such treatment centers in the United States" at the time.[4]

A hundred years ago, Father Judge, who saw things "truly from a spiritual perspective that is impractical in a more worldly sense," also had a vision about the enormous role the laity would need to play to grow the Church.[5] He expressed it succinctly: "Every Catholic an Apostle." With tremendous trust in divine providence and inspired heavily by Saint Vincent de Paul, the patron saint of charitable societies, Father Judge believed in cultivating an informed and highly spiritualized laity to tend to otherwise abandoned work.[6] He was equally as enthusiastic about the preservation of the Faith, working to gather laywomen to keep the Faith alive in African-American and Italian immigrant communities in New York. He understood that with the Church as our Mother, Catholics are obliged to perform regular corporal and spiritual acts of mercy as the Body of Christ.

Father Judge's charism motivates me on a daily basis. Every moment of every day, we're called to share the Good News of the Gospel. *Lumen Gentium* called this the "universal call to holiness." Whatever moniker one applies to this concept, it's powerful — it's of the utmost importance. When we wake up in the morning, we can be confident that the work we do that day is no less than what the Apostles were called to do.

God called me to spread that message to those suffering from addictions and their families. But wherever people are sick and suffering, every Catholic is called to respond with mercy and compassion.

Be Doers, Not Hearers Only

As Catholics, we are called to recognize the pain and suffering in our brothers and sisters and to walk with them in it. We are tasked with being like Christ, who listened to the aching, touched the leper, and embraced the sinner. This means that if someone's making a bad decision, we don't only look at the decision itself, but ask why they're making that decision. We invest time and energy in understanding what's hurting that person so desperately. This much is simply the Gospel. And while I can appreciate not understanding addiction — the impetus for the preceding chapters of this book — what I don't understand is refusing to see the pain behind the decision-making.

I repost a lot of articles on LinkedIn: about the iatrogenic nature of the opioid crisis, how people have suffered in coming out of the pandemic, and so on. My connections on this platform are usually not people I know in person. Rather, they are lay leaders of other ministries and individuals working in Catholic media. I use social media in my great hope that such folks will want to join the work of the Church by taking an active role in this situation.

One evening, I received an email alerting me of a reply to one of my postings. I started to read the message, which came from an older Catholic woman with a prominent position within the Church. She wrote that addiction was a choice, a moral failing, and she went on to explain why the US attempt at Prohibition didn't work.

Bewildered, I chose to go straight to bed.

Before falling asleep, I mentally composed what I thought was a succinct and erudite response. The gist was this: I get it. If you have not been touched by or have not loved someone who has suffered, if you are not educated in what addiction is as a disease of mind, body, and spirit, I can understand making these kinds of comments. But as a Catholic, how can you not see the pain at the root of these choices? If someone is making a choice that separates him from God, family, and community, what tremendous suffering must he be enduring? Shouldn't we respond to the pain that could send someone into the abyss of addiction? The impetus might have been the person's attempt to assuage the pain of trauma or abuse, or it might have been that person's misguided effort to fit in and find their herd. Sometimes their choice was a grasp for confidence. Other times it was curiosity that became a compulsion. Sometimes the origin was just getting a tooth pulled. In any of these scenarios, ought we not to tend to this misdirection, this falling off course?

By the grace of God, I wasn't able to publish my response. When I returned to my LinkedIn post the next day, her comment had disappeared. Thank God it wasn't even up for twelve hours. Maybe someone else responded to it first, or perhaps the Blessed Mother interceded on behalf of the suffering.

But the experience of reading her perspective brought home to me yet again that we, as a Church, are still walking away from too many people. It's disheartening to see those who espouse Catholicism — whether as a public figure or not, but even more so in the former case — stop short of asking why someone would make a painful choice that excludes them from community and sends them on a desolate path. Are we not called to tend to this sign of spiritual disease, to help remediate the situation by reaching out, by being present, by offering to be a companion on the journey? Whatever brings someone to this point, we have to be there without judgment.

Be Like Christ, Who Came for Sinners

Let's not forget what Father Zack explained: Every soul, no matter its state on earth, is one with whom God desires to spend eternity. In the First Letter to Timothy, Saint Paul writes:

> The saying is sure and worthy of full acceptance, that Christ Jesus came into the world to save sinners. And I am the foremost of sinners; but I received mercy for this reason, that in me, as the foremost, Jesus Christ might display his perfect patience for an example to those who were to believe in him for eternal life. (1:15–16)

This message, this love, and this mercy are for everyone. Christ came for sinners; he ate with them time and again. Yet time and again, we twenty-first-century Catholics judge the sinner and turn our backs. We espouse one thing and do something else. We need to eliminate this discrepancy from the way we live our lives, for the good of our brothers and sisters and for the future of the Church.

Of course, not every Catholic fails to understand the mercy we are called to show the sick and suffering. So many are dedicated to this work. So many work with other marginalized populations. Consider those who work with unwed expectant mothers, who care for mother and baby through pregnancy, delivery, and afterward until both are ready to stand on their own feet. Think of the doctors, nurses, and others who volunteer their time to bring *malades* to bathe in the waters at Lourdes. Look at my own brothers in the Missionary Servants of the Most Holy Trinity, who serve the traditionally underserved or underheard, the poorest of the poor, on two different continents.

These works make a difference, but so do the small, meaningful sacrifices and acts of generosity that ordinary people undertake in the providence of their daily lives. Love and compassion are shown not only in bigger works, those that might feel overwhelming to many of us, but also in seemingly little acts done with intention.

So many of the saints — many of them named Teresa or the equivalent — have expressed this truth in their own words. Saint Thérèse of Lisieux professed that "Jesus does not ask for great deeds, but only for gratitude and self-surrender."[7] Saint Teresa of Calcutta is remembered for her proclamation that we ought to do small things with great love, and that if we want peace in the world, we ought to go home and love our families. Saint Teresa of Avila reminds us that God moves amidst the pots and pans. However one puts it, the point is that we need to reach out to people, to be present, to welcome the opportunity to participate in another's journey. When we allow the scope of our daily lives to include cooperation as a community, these little things start to make big changes.

Saint Paul wrote in his First Letter to the Corinthians: "Now there are varieties of gifts, but the same Spirit; and there are varieties of service, but the same Lord; and there are varieties of working, but it is the same God who inspires them all in every one. To each is given the manifestation of the Spirit for the common good" (12:4–7). To begin, we must identify the gifts the Lord has given us — and I assure you that for each of us, there are many. Then we need to ask God how he desires for us to put them to work.

His answer is probably going to mean getting out of our comfort zones. He's probably going to require us to be stretched in ways we've avoided until now. But it's said that charity isn't charity unless you feel it. Proper gratitude for the gifts the Lord has given us looks like asking, time and again, where and how we can serve in our homes, in our parishes, in our workplaces, in our schools, and then following through.

Every morning I pray for a holy inconvenience, for something that will humble me and interrupt my plans. I ask for something to give me an opportunity to surrender my will to the Lord's. I pray that I will have the grace to keep saying yes, to keep giving my fiat each day, and to do so with joy. When I feel that I'm giving beyond what I can spare, like the widow who gave her mite in the temple offering, then I know that my prayer was answered.

Be Good. Do Good. Be a Power for Good.

Father Judge famously said, "Be good. Do good. Be a power for good." He understood that every one of us can be a missionary in the providence of our daily lives: in the workplace, in the home, in line at the grocery store.

First, we need to be good. We need to tend to our own spiritual lives with honesty and sincerity. We need to focus ourselves on him who is the Source and, in that way, to eliminate distractions from our daily lives. How do we focus on the Source? Through prayer and meditation, through active and regular participation in the sacramental life of the Church. We must make it a priority to cultivate a personal relationship with the Lord through prayer.

Then, we need to do good. We need to seek opportunities to be present to others, especially in these times of great personal and societal turmoil. We need to be aware of and acknowledge our neighbor's suffering and fears and then reach out in kindness with open heart and open ears. We need to engage in the art of accompaniment and the culture of encounter. Pope Francis believes we can best recover the culture of encounter through "awakening the capacity for dialogue."[8] In a speech in Buenos Aires, he said:

> When one recovers the outward focus of the encounter, one begins to dialogue, and this means not only *hearing* but recovering the ability to *listen*. The other person, even if ideologically, politically, or socially on the opposing side, always has something good to give me, and I always have something good to give him. At that encounter, from which I draw good things, we can build a creative and fruitful synthesis. The dialogue is fundamentally fruitful; monologues lose their way.[9]

Finally, we need to be a power for good. My ninety-five-year-old father lives this mantra beautifully. At the beginning of the COVID-19 pandemic, my mother passed away, one month shy of their seventieth wedding anniversary (for the record, she did not die from COVID-19). She was ninety-one. I was worried about my father, because during the last years of their lives together, he had assumed the role of caregiver as her Alzheimer's worsened. Now that he didn't have that responsibility, I didn't know if he would thrive or if he would linger for a short while and that would be it.

As it turns out, thanks be to God, he thrived. After he no longer needed to serve my mom, the Holy Spirit gave him a new mission, and he set about living it with his whole heart. The women who took care of my mother became his companions. Two had been baptized in the Faith but were not practicing. Early on, he invited them to begin praying the Rosary with him, something they hadn't done before. Now they pray with him every day, and they carry into their own families the hope and joy that comes from this devotion. When a Eucharistic minister comes weekly to bring him Communion, they take Communion too. Not only that, but *he* cooks for *them*!

My father chose not to get complacent or comfortable, as understandable as that would have been at his age and in his situation. His new mission is a mission of evangelization. He is a messenger of the Good News of Jesus Christ. He wakes up each morning with this purpose, which gives his life abundance and joy.

So here's the challenge: If he can do it at age ninety-five, how are you going to be a missionary, an apostle in your daily life?

Reflect

- Fr. Thomas Judge's motto, "Every Catholic an Apostle," is a call to action for all to be messengers of the Good News of Jesus Christ. What opportunities do you have, in the providence of your daily life, to act as a missionary?
- Too often, the disease of addiction is misunderstood and therefore stigmatized. How would you describe the afflicted person's pain to someone who has no experience with addiction? How might you help them understand why we are called to extend Christ's love and mercy to all his suffering children?
- Father Judge not only believed that it is incumbent upon us to be good and to do good, but challenged us to be a power for good. What does "Be a power for good" mean for you? How might you live that

out in your own life?

Pray

My Lord and my God, you alone are the Source of all things good on this earth. Help me to be good, to do good, and to be a power for good for all those whom I meet in the providence of my daily life.

Help me to understand that I, too, am a missionary, spreading the Good News of your love and mercy to all whom I meet, wherever I meet them.

Let me journey, as an apostle of love, both to the margins to reach those who have been abandoned and to those in my own home or workplace.

Wherever I go, whomever I'm with, let all see in me a reflection of you and of your infinite love. In Christ's name, I pray.

Amen.

❧

Conclusion
Quenching His Thirst and Empowering the Church

I see in your suffering face, my son, the Face of Jesus, my Beloved. And I hear your words cry out, echoing him, "I was thirsty, and you gave me something to drink." I take your hand in mine and place it also in Jesus' hand — bound we are now — "a threefold cord is not quickly broken." I am loving you as you lay on the floor of your life and I cry out, "This is my beloved son" to Jesus, the Son of God, in prayer.

And I am remembering Abraham's response to Isaac on the way to the altar of sacrifice — "God will provide" — as I trust that my sacrificial love of you will allow the procreation of all the grace needed for you to survive this trial.

> *I see you there, my son, in the throes of darkness, star-*
> *ing back at me with the eyes of Christ. My heart holds you*
> *there, a pieta of love and sorrow, as I pick you up and help*
> *you carry your cross. You see, I am your Simon of Cyrene,*
> *and I will help you carry this burden.*
>
> — *Lynn*

We read in the first pericope of Psalm 42:

As a deer longs for flowing streams,
so longs my soul
for you, O God.
My soul thirsts for God,
for the living God.
When shall I come and behold
the face of God? (42:1–2)

In reflecting on these verses, Pope St. John Paul II equated the thirsting deer with "the praying person who tends with his whole being, body and soul, towards the Lord, who seems distant and yet very much needed."[1] The pain expressed by the writer of Psalm 42 — perhaps David in exile or someone from the king-dom of Israel who was being kept away from Jerusalem and the temple there — is the pain of being separated from community and longing for spiritual healing. *Nephesh*, the word for "soul" in this passage, can also mean "throat," and so we see the desire to be satiated, quenched, by living water.

These words about being isolated from worshiping in commu-nity and experiencing a deep longing for God might just as keenly be felt by someone suffering through a pandemic or by someone isolated and ostracized because of addiction. Sacred Scripture

proves that this isolation is not new. Many of our spiritual ancestors have already gone through the turmoil we're experiencing in
the present day. They allowed their own unnatural attachments to
distract them from a deeper intimacy with God, their fellows, and
themselves. And time and again, God stepped in with his grace
and his promise that if they — if we — would return to him with
a contrite heart, he would welcome us back home.

Sometimes the journey home is daunting and frightening,
because the transition from the abyss of addiction to the life
and light of recovery can be scary and painful. The feelings of
unworthiness that so many of our contemporaries suffer under
make up such a heavy burden. In reflecting on pain and suffering, Anna Lembke writes, "Ironically, as our lives have become
progressively more comfortable, with modernization, increased
leisure time, and decreased threat of illness and injury, we have
become less and less able to tolerate any kind of pain."[2] Pain is,
frankly, part of life. It's not something we can escape, and while
we shouldn't try to bring it on ourselves, we also shouldn't run
away from it. It is in our brokenness that we are made whole. It
is in our sins that we are redeemed. It is in our wounds that we
find connection and communion with one another and with the
Lord, our God. We're all on the same journey, and the goal for us
all is heaven. Third-century Christian writer Origen wrote with
timeless wisdom when he "explained that the human search for
God is a never-ending venture because progress is ever possible
and necessary."[3]

Whether or not you have a story of recovery, whether or not
you're a trained companion or a professional counselor, if you
have a deep and abiding desire to care for the spiritual condition
of your neighbor, there's a place for you in this work. We all have
a role to play in finding meaning and purpose in our own lives
and helping others to do the same.

We have this obligation to respond to our brothers and sisters on the margins, those who dwell, as Father Judge reminds us, in the tangled portions of the Vineyard. To do so, we must empower our Church to become a resource for those suffering from addictions and their families.

An empowered Church needs boots on the ground in every parish.

An empowered Church needs servant leaders.

An empowered Church needs to remember how to create disciples.

An empowered Church needs to have an amplified voice in the midst of great societal maladies.

An empowered Church needs to insist that her voice is heard.

It's hard to hear, but the reality is that your church has an addiction problem. Your school has an addiction problem. Your workplace has an addiction problem.

What are you going to do about it?

Acknowledgments

Many thanks to all the Missionary Servants of the Most Holy Trinity who have given me a platform and a voice in helping serve those with addictions, especially Fr. Michael Barth, ST; Br. Joe Dudek, ST; Fr. Luis De La Cuadra, ST; Fr. Jesus Ramirez, ST; Br. John Skrodinsky, ST; and Fr. Dennis Berry. I would also like to thank John Butler, Vice President of Mission Advancement, for his guidance and belief that our work could make a difference in the Church.

Many thanks to all those who welcomed me as part of the retreat team at the Shrine of St. Joseph, where I discovered my passion for working with those suffering from addictions, especially the late Ron and Dolly Reinhart, Ray and Rose Cody, Ray and Bea Makara, Sr. Andre Dembowski, and Grace Wamsteker.

Many thanks to Seton Hall University and those at the Immaculate Conception Seminary School of Theology, Department of Continuing Education and Professional Studies, and CORE Curriculum, who have supported both my academic and professional efforts, especially Dr. Dianne Traflet, Dr. Gregory Glazov, Dr. Julie Burkey, former Dean Karen Passaro, former Associate Dean Diane Russo, Dr. Nancy Enright, and Professor Melinda Papaccio.

Many thanks to Sean Cardinal O'Malley and the Archdiocese of Boston, specifically members of the Archdiocesan Opioid Task Force, who test-piloted the iTHIRST program, most notably Joe McEnness, Fr. Joe White, Deacon Jim Greer, and Doreen Rearden. Thanks also to Mother Olga Yaqob of the Sacred Heart and the Daughters of Mary of Nazareth for their support, hospitality, and commitment to serving the most vulnerable among us.

Many thanks to Melinda, James, Mosadi-Rra, Deirdre, Sara, Blitch, Fr. Mike Barth, and Lynn for sharing their thoughtful narratives at the beginning of each chapter. Your stories touch our hearts. Thanks also to Fr. Zachary Swantek for his generosity in sharing his theological expertise, especially as it concerns the Theology of the Body.

Many thanks to John, the young man whose struggle inspired me to begin this journey to help those who suffer from addiction. May you always find the peace and joy that a focus on Christ will provide, and may you continue to be blessed along your own Road to Hope.

Many thanks to the team at Our Sunday Visitor who shared my vision for what this book could be and helped bring it to fruition. I am especially grateful to Mary Beth Giltner, Rebecca Martin, and Jeanette Fast Redmond, as well as Neal Quandt and Zach Silka. Thanks also go to Alexandra Penfold of Upstart Crow Literary Agency for her guidance.

Many thanks to my parish priest, Fr. Wayne Varga, and Deacon Wayne von Doehren for their constant support and prayers. Thanks also to all who have helped keep my home and farm running smoothly when I needed time to write, especially Elizabeth (Chris) Higgins, the late Richard Stopa, Barbara Longeri, and Allison Bergin Gaspari.

Many thanks to my friend and coauthor, Lindsay Schlegel, who gave order and direction to my passionate words regarding the Church's role in the opioid epidemic. Your guidance and your friendship have become invaluable to me. Thanks also to Allan Wright for connecting us and for believing in the words I felt called to share.

Many thanks to all the iTHIRST Team serving the vulnerable and marginalized across the country and beyond. I am humbled by your dedication to our work.

Last but certainly not least, many thanks to my husband, Thomas Petronaci, and son, Michael Giancarlo Orrico, for their unending support throughout all my careers. You have my heart.

Appendix
Our Cloud of Witnesses

In the Letter to the Hebrews, we read, "Therefore, since we are surrounded by so great a cloud of witnesses, let us also lay aside every weight, and sin which clings so closely, and let us run with perseverance the race that is set before us, looking to Jesus the pioneer and perfecter of our faith" (Heb 12:1–2). The "cloud of witnesses" is the communion of saints: those men, women, and children who have gone before us in faith and now sit before the throne of grace, ready and willing to intercede for us. The holy people listed here are but a few of those to whom you can look for assistance on your journey to be the face of Christ for those who are sick and suffering.

The Blessed Virgin Mary, Mother of Us All

In one of his last actions before his death, Christ gave his mother to be our mother. Mary loves each of the children of God with a mother's love. Coronated as Queen of Heaven and Earth, she desires to intercede for those in need of mercy. Many Catholics choose to consecrate, that is, dedicate, themselves to the Blessed Mother, entrusting themselves to her prayer and protection. Here is my favorite daily prayer of consecration, written by St. Louis de Montfort: "I deliver and consecrate to thee, as thy slave, my body and soul, my goods, both interior and exterior, and even the value of all my good actions past, present and future; leaving to thee the entire and full right of disposing of me, and all that belongs to me, without exception, according to thy good pleasure, for the greater glory of God, in time and in eternity. Amen."

Saint Joseph, Our Blessed Mother's Most Chaste Spouse

Any number of the titles in the Litany of Saint Joseph attest to his relevance to and patronage of the work we do in substance use disorder recovery: "Mirror of patience, Lover of poverty … Cornerstone of families, Support in difficulties, Comfort of the sorrowing, Hope of the sick, Patron of exiles, Patron of the afflicted, Patron of the poor, Patron of the dying, Terror of demons."[1] Saint Joseph is our protector, and we can trust he will guard us in our work with the same love, intentionality, and grace with which he guarded Jesus and the Blessed Virgin Mary.

Patrons for Those Dealing with Substance Use Challenges

Saint Maximilian Kolbe,
Patron Saint of IV Drug Users

St. Maximilian Kolbe was a Polish Catholic priest who died in Auschwitz in 1941. He volunteered himself to take the place of another man sentenced to death and was subjected to death by starvation with nine other men. Some reports posit that two weeks later, he was the only one alive. Others state that three weeks into the torture, he and three others were still alive. Either way, the guards wanted whoever remained dead, and they brought that to pass through a lethal injection of carbolic acid.[2] Due to his cause of death, therefore, Saint Maximilian is the patron saint of those addicted to drugs. He is also the patron saint of families, prisoners, the pro-life movement, and, per Pope St. John Paul II, "the patron saint of our difficult century" (then the twentieth century, but we can just as easily invoke him for the twenty-first century as well). Saint Maximilian Kolbe had an intense devotion to the Blessed Mother and was the founder of the Militia of the Immaculata, "whose aim was to fight evil with the witness of the good life, prayer, work, and suffering."[3]

Saint Mark Ji Tianxiang,
Patron Saint of Those Addicted to Drugs

Saint Mark Ji Tianxiang was a devout Chinese doctor who treated the poor for free. He also suffered from addiction to opium and was martyred along with his family during the Boxer Rebellion in 1900.[4] Like many of those who suffer from substance use disorders today, Saint Ji began using opium to treat a medical condition (in his case, a stomach ailment) and became addicted. He tried many times to stop using, but he never recovered from his addiction. Because addiction was not understood then as we are beginning to understand it now, Ji — believing himself to be too sinful   abstained from receiving the Eucharist for 30 years, while continuing to practice the Faith, even amidst persecution"[5] to the point of death. When he and his family were brought to the site of their execution, he insisted on dying last, so that none of his children or grandchildren would have to die alone. And all the time, he sang the Litany of Our Lady.[6]

Venerable Matthew Talbot,
Patron of Alcoholics, Sobriety, and Recovery from Substance Use and Addictions

Venerable Matthew Talbot began drinking when he was a young teenager, and he suffered from alcoholism for fifteen years.[7] When he decided to stop drinking, he made a general confession and started to attend daily Mass. He was in recovery for the rest of his life, though the first seven years of sobriety were particularly challenging. He lived a life of penance, prayer (especially praying the Rosary — here we see Mother Mary yet again), and generous almsgiving. He died in 1925.

Other Helpful Patrons

Saint Monica and Saint Augustine,
The Mother-Son Dream Team

Maybe one conversion story is more dramatic than Father Callo-way's, or at least on par with it. As a young man, Saint Augustine lived a life of sin and rejection of God, chronicled in his *Confessions*, before his conversion. His mother, Saint Monica, prayed and fasted with perseverance for seventeen years prior to her son's change of heart. While hers is a beautiful example of the power of prayer, praying hard enough for a family member of course cannot guarantee a turn in our loved one's life. Each of us has free will to choose or reject grace. But we can pray for those who are afflicted to open their hearts to the Lord, and we can do that through the intercession of Saint Monica, patron of alcoholics, mothers, and wives, and her son, Saint Augustine, Doctor of the Church.

Saint Teresa of Avila,
Doctor of the Church and Patron of the Sick

I was in my forties when I had the spiritual revelation that led to the work I do today. I was inspired to write by Saint Teresa of Avila, who was also in her forties when she reformed her Carmelite order. Saint Teresa reminds me that we are called to continuous conversion. Her writings on mental prayer and meditation contributed to her designation as a Doctor of the Church. Four hundred years later, her wisdom continues to guide souls back home to Christ.

Dorothy Day,
Founder of the Catholic Worker Movement

The cause for Dorothy Day's sainthood has been formally opened, but it remains in an early stage as of the writing of this book. Whether or not she is ultimately canonized as a Catholic saint, she is a modern-day person who saw the face of Christ in the underserved and the underheard. She recognized herself as flawed and was willing to embrace those flaws, which makes her so relatable. Even in admitting her flaws, she still desired, beyond all things, to make the journey closer to Christ and to take others with her.

Day lived, loved, and suffered the pain of loss in relationship. She's like a Mary Magdalene figure; she understood Christ perhaps better than many others because of what she endured. Day's first book, *From Union Square to Rome,* was originally published by Preservation Press, the publishing arm of the Missionary Servants of the Most Holy Trinity. Her editor, Fr. Joachim Benson, wrote, "It is very easy to see how much the Missionary Servants and the Catholic Workers have in common," and he cited the publication and promotion of Day's book as "one of my missionary activities."[8]

Notes

Introduction

1. Substance Abuse and Mental Health Services Administration, *Key substance use and mental health indicators in the United States: Results from the 2018 National Survey on Drug Use and Health* (Rockville: Center for Behavioral Health Statistics and Quality, Substance Abuse and Mental Health Services Administration, 2019).

2. Gerald G. May, *Addiction and Grace: Love and Spirituality in the Healing of Addictions* (New York: HarperOne, 1988), 1.

3. Ibid.

4. Ibid., 3.

5. Ibid.

6. Ibid.

7. Ibid., 4.

8. Ibid.

9. Centers for Disease Control and Prevention/National Center for Health Statistics, "Drug Overdose Deaths in the U. S. Top 100,000 Annually," November 17, 2021, https://www.cdc.gov/nchs/pressroom/nchs_press_releases/2021/20211117.htm.

10. Francis, Chrism Mass homily, March 28, 2013, vatican.va.

Chapter 1

1. Henri J. M. Nouwen, "The Wounded Healer," *Henri Nouwen Society,* July 8, 2018, https://henrinouwen.org/meditations/the-wounded-healer/.

2. May, *Addiction and Grace*, 17.

3. Teresa of Calcutta, *Missionaries of Charity*, https://www.motherteresa.org/missionaries-of-charity.html.

4. May, *Addiction and Grace*, 12.

5. Robert Barron, *Catholicism: A Journey to the Heart of the Faith* (New York: Image Books, 2011), 43.

6. Ibid.

7. May, *Addiction and Grace*, 14.

8. Ibid., 24–25.

9. Ibid, 26–29.

10. Ibid, 124–125.

Chapter 2

1. "The Six Dimensions of Wellness," National Wellness Institute, https://nationalwellness.org/resources/six-dimensions-of-wellness/.

2. Ibid.

3. Bill Wilson, *Alcoholics Anonymous Comes of Age: A Brief History of A. A.* (New York: Alcoholics Anonymous World Services, 1957), 167.

4. Beth Macy, *Dopesick: Dealers, Doctors, and the Drug Company that Addicted America* (New York: Back Bay Books, 2019), 21–22, 25, 30.

5. Ibid., 27.

6. Anna Lembke, *Drug Dealer, MD: How Doctors Were Duped, Patients Got Hooked, and Why It's So Hard to Stop* (Baltimore, MD: Johns Hopkins University Press, 2016), 41.

7. Ibid., 42.

8. Ibid.

9. Ibid., 66.

10. Macy, *Dopesick*, 20-21.

11. Ibid., 95.

12. Ibid., 47.

13. Lembke, *Drug Dealer, MD*, 57.

14. Macy, *Dopesick*, 52.

15. Ibid., 107.

16. Lembke, *Drug Dealer, MD*, 79.

17. Ibid., 74.

18. Macy, *Dopesick*, 41.

19. Lembke, *Drug Dealer, MD*, 81.

20. Ibid.

21. Name changed to protect privacy.

22. Gerald G. May, *Will and Spirit: A Contemplative Psychology* (New York: Harper Collins, 1982), 291.

23. Francis, Holy Mass for the Closing of the XV Ordinary General Assembly of the Synod of Bishops, homily, October 28, 2018, vatican .va.

Chapter 3

1. Francis, general audience, August 28, 2019, vatican.va.

2. Brandon Vogt, "St. Lawrence and the True Treasures of the Church," *Word on Fire*, https://www.wordonfire.org/resources /blog/st-lawrence-and-the-true-treasures-of-the-church/4878/.

3. "Spiritual Awareness/Awakening Quotes," *Jesuit Resource*, https:// www.xavier.edu/jesuitresource/online-resources/quote-archive1 /spiritual-awareness-quotes.

4. Zachary Swantek, in conversation with the authors, January 2022.

5. Benedict XVI, *Deus Caritas Est*, December 25, 2005, vatican .va, sec. 18.

6. Paul VI, *Gaudium et Spes*, December 7, 1965, vatican.va, sec. 24.

Chapter 4

1. Francis, "Communication and Mercy: A Fruitful Encounter," January 24, 2016, vatican.va.

2. Francis, "Meeting with Young People," February 16, 2016, vatican. va.

3. Thomas Augustine Judge, *Missionary Cenacle Meditations* (Philadelphia, PA: Missionary Cenacle Press, 1998), 235.

4. Neel Burton, "Empathy vs. Sympathy," *Psychology Today*, May 22, 2015, updated April 27, 2020, https://www.psychologytoday.com/us/blog /hide-and-seek/201505/empathy-vs-sympathy.

5. Francis, *Evangelii Gaudium*, November 24, 2013, vatican.va, sec. 170.

6. Ibid., sec. 171.

7. Judge, *Missionary Cenacle Meditations*, 9.

Chapter 5

1. Lembke, *Drug Dealer, MD*, 40.

2. Ibid., 40–41.

3. Thomas Merton, *The Wisdom of the Desert* (New York: New Directions, 1970), LXXXIX.

4. Amy Peterson, "Golden Scars," *Our Daily Bread*, October 20, 2020, https://odb.org/US/2020/10/20/golden-scars.

5. John Paul II, *Salvifici Doloris*, vatican.va, sec. 3. Emphasis in original.

6. Ibid., sec. 19.

7. Richard G. Tedeschi and Lawrence G. Calhoun, "Posttraumatic Growth: Conceptual Foundations and Empirical Evidence," *Psychological Inquiry* 15, no. 1 (2004): 1–18. http://www.jstor.org/stable/20447194.

8. Marcia Wakeland, "The Art of Listening Deeply with the Vulnerable and Marginalized," *Presence: An International Journal of Spiritual Direction*, June 2017, 27–33.

9. Faustina Maria Pia, *Jesus, I Trust in You: A 30-Day Personal Retreat with the Litany of Trust* (Steubenville, OH: Emmaus Road Publishing, 2021), 76.

10. Wakeland, "The Art of Listening Deeply."

Chapter 6

1. Nathan Yerby, "Statistics On Addiction In America," *Addiction Center*, https://www.addictioncenter.com/addiction/addiction-statistics/.

2. Ibid.

3. National Center for Drug Abuse Statistics, "Drug Abuse Statistics," https://drugabusestatistics.org/.

4. Patrick Carnes, *A Gentle Path through the Twelve Steps: The Classic Guide for All People in the Process of Recovery* (Minneapolis, MN: Hazelden, 2012), 21.

5. Juan Luis Bastero, *Mary, Mother of the Redeemer*, trans. Michael

Adams and Philip Griffin (Portland, OR: Four Courts Press, 2006), 18.

6. Ibid.

7. Donald H. Calloway, *No Turning Back: A Witness to Mercy* (Stockbridge, MA: Marian Press, 2018), 159.

8. Ibid., 162.

9. Ibid., 184.

10. Name changed to protect privacy.

Chapter 7

1. Carl J. Ganz, *St. Joseph's Shrine, Stirling, New Jersey: A Centennial History 1924–2024* (South Orange, NJ: New Jersey Catholic Historical Commission, 2022).

2. Ibid.

3. Ibid.

4. Ibid.

5. William L. Portier, *Every Catholic an Apostle: A Life of Thomas A. Judge, CM, 1868–1933* (Washington, D.C.: The Catholic University of America Press, 2017), 523.

6. Ibid.

7. Thérèse of Lisieux, *Story of a Soul* (Huntington, IN: Our Sunday Visitor, 2018), 151.

8. Cardinal Jorge Mario Bergoglio, *Encountering Christ* (New Rochelle, NY: Scepter, 2013), 138.

9. Ibid.

Conclusion

1. John Paul II, general audience, January 16, 2002, vatican.va, sec. 2.

2. Lembke, *Drug Dealer*, 43.

3. John Paul II, general audience, sec. 2.

Appendix

1. "Litany of St. Joseph," *United States Conference of Catholic Bishops*, https://www.usccb.org/prayers/litany-saint-joseph.

2. Ellyn von Huben, "9 Things to Know about St. Maximilian Kolbe," *Word on Fire,* https://www.wordonfire.org/articles/9-things-to-know-about-st-maximilian-kolbe/.

3. "Saint Maximilian Mary Kolbe," *Franciscan Media,* https://www.franciscanmedia.org/saint-of-the-day/saint-maximilian-mary-kolbe.

4. Catholic News Agency, "How This Catholic Saint Might Be the Patron of Opioid Addicts," *Angelus News,* https://angelusnews.com/faith/how-this-catholic-saint-might-be-the-patron-of-opioid-addicts/.

5. Ibid.

6. Hugh Barbour, O. Praem., "Addict, Martyr, and Saint," *Catholic Answers,* https://www.catholic.com/audio/caf/st-mark-ji-tianxiang-addict-martyr-and-saint.

7. "Venerable Matt Talbot," *Franciscan Media,* https://www.franciscanmedia.org/saint-of-the-day/venerable-matt-talbot.

8. Portier, *Every Catholic an Apostle,* 525.

Further Reading

First and foremost, I recommend regular reading of Sacred Scripture. I prefer the New American Bible–Revised Edition (NABRE) or the Revised Standard Version–Catholic Edition of the Bible (RSVCE). The full text of the NABRE is available at the website of the United States Conference of Catholic Bishops. The NABRE is the text of the Lectionary, which is used for Mass in the United States. If you're not sure where to start, try the three sections on which Twelve Step programs are founded: the Sermon on the Mount (Mt 5–7), 1 Cor 13, and the Letter of James.

The resources below are foundational to our work at iTHIRST. Some deal with the intersection of spirituality, addiction, and recovery. Others explore the origin of the opioid crisis itself. Given in alphabetical order by title, these selections can expand your knowledge of the disease of addiction as you seek to respond in your parish community and beyond.

Addiction & Grace: Love and Spirituality in the Healing of Addictions by Gerald G. May

This watershed book discusses the interface between addiction and spirituality, which has often been ignored in a clinical setting. If you want to understand this connection, this is the best place to begin.

Alcoholics Anonymous Comes of Age: A Brief History of A. A. by Bill Wilson

Also known as "The Big Book of AA," this volume is probably the greatest work regarding addiction ever written from the perspective of the person suffering. It is truly inspired by the Holy Spirit.

Daily Companion for Healing Addictions by Allan Wright
This great daily devotional supports those afflicted by addiction and their loved ones. Each day's entry includes a reflection, Scripture or quote, and prayer.

Dopesick: Dealers, Doctors, and the Drug Company That Addicted America by Beth Macy
Macy combines elements of investigative reporting and biographical narrative to chronicle how drug companies — Purdue Pharma, in particular — targeted low-income people in socio-economically underdeveloped areas of the nation and took advantage of an already hurting population.

Drug Dealer, MD: How Doctors Were Duped, Patients Got Hooked and Why It's So Hard to Stop by Anna Lembke
Lembke's research gives a realistic view of the role that physicians have sometimes unwittingly played in the progression of an iatrogenic catastrophe. This history also explores the involvement of academic institutions, regulatory agencies, and more.

Every Catholic an Apostle: A Life of Thomas A. Judge, CM, 1868–1933 by William L. Portier
This resource is the most comprehensive discussion of this contemporary Vincentian, whose life and legacy continue to affect people today. It chronicles how Father Judge encouraged the participation of laity as apostles and goes into detail about the four communities he founded.

No Turning Back: A Witness to Mercy
by Fr. Donald Calloway, MIC
Fr. Donald Calloway's journey to the Faith, never mind to the priesthood, is nothing short of miraculous, and his account encourages the reader to be persistent in praying even for what

seem the most desperate cases. In this memoir, he recounts how lost he was as a promiscuous and addicted adolescent and young man, as well as how profound the mercy he experienced was in his conversion.

The Big Hustle: A Boston Street Kid's Story of Addiction and Redemption by Jim Wahlberg

Wahlberg pens a poignant memoir about his descent into addiction as an adolescent son of an alcoholic father and an overwhelmed mother. At age twenty-two, he was sentenced to nine years in prison, and it was there — through the intercession of a Catholic priest and a surprise visit from Mother Teresa — that he began his journey of faith and recovery.

The Twelve Steps and the Sacraments: A Catholic Journey through Recovery by Scott Weeman

In this and the accompanying workbook, Weeman weaves a deep understanding of the sacramental life of the Church together with a profound knowledge of the spirituality of addiction and recovery in what can only be described as a true tapestry of love and healing.

What Pope Francis Says About Recovery: 30 Days of Reflections and Prayers (booklet) by Twenty-Third Publications

This small volume offers beautiful, moving reflections from the Holy Father on our marginalized brothers and sisters. It's a book for anyone who has a heart to serve those who are suffering and will be particularly helpful for those afflicted and their families.

Bibliography

Barbour, Hugh, O. Praem. "Addict, Martyr, and Saint." Catholic
   Answers. https://www.catholic.com/audio/caf/st-mark
   -ji-tianxiang-addict-martyr-and-saint.

Barron, Robert. *Catholicism: A Journey to the Heart of the Faith.*
   New York: Image Books, 2011.

Bastero, Juan Luis. *Mary, Mother of the Redeemer.* Trans. Michael
   Adams and Philip Griffin. Portland, OR: Four Courts
   Press, 2006.

Benedict XVI, Pope. *Deus Caritas Est.* Encyclical Letter. December 25, 2005. vatican.va.

Bergoglio, Cardinal Jorge Mario. *Encountering Christ.* New
   Rochelle, NY: Scepter, 2013.

Burton, Neel. "Empathy vs. Sympathy." *Psychology Today.* May 22,
   2015, updated April 27, 2020. https://www
   .psychologytoday.com/us/blog/hide-and-seek/201505
   /empathy-vs-sympathy.

Calloway, Donald H. *No Turning Back: A Witness to Mercy.* Stockbridge MA: Marian Press, 2018.

Carnes, Patrick. *A Gentle Path through the Twelve Steps: The Classic Guide for All People in the Process of Recovery.* Minneapolis: Hazelden, 2012.

Catholic News Agency. "How This Catholic Saint Might Be the
   Patron of Opioid Addicts." Angelus News. https://
   angelusnews.com/faith/how-this-catholic-saint-might
   -be-the-patron-of-opioid-addicts/.

Centers for Disease Control and Prevention/National Center for Health Statistics. "Drug Overdose Deaths in
   the U. S. Top 100,000 Annually." November 17, 2021.
   https://www.cdc.gov/nchs/pressroom/nchs_press

_releases/2021/20211117.htm.

Francis, Pope. Chrism Mass Homily. March 28, 2013. vatican.va.

Francis, Pope. "Communication and Mercy: A Fruitful Encounter." January 24, 2016. vatican.va.

Francis, Pope. *Evangelii Gaudium*. Apostolic Exhortation. November 24, 2013. vatican.va.

Francis, Pope. General Audience. August 28, 2019. vatican.va.

Francis, Pope. Holy Mass for the Closing of the XV Ordinary General Assembly of the Synod of Bishops. Homily. October 28, 2018. vatican.va.

Francis, Pope. "Meeting with Young People." February 16, 2016. vatican.va.

Ganz, Carl J. *St. Joseph's Shrine, Stirling, New Jersey: A Centennial History 1924-2024*. South Orange, NJ: New Jersey Catholic Historical Commission, 2022.

John Paul II, Pope. General Audience. January 16, 2002. vatican.va.

John Paul II, Pope. *Salvifici Doloris*. Apostolic Letter. vatican.va.

Judge, Thomas Augustine. *Missionary Cenacle Meditations*. Philadelphia, PA: Missionary Cenacle Press, 1998.

Lembke, Anna. *Drug Dealer, MD: How Doctors Were Duped, Patients Got Hooked and Why It's So Hard to Stop*. Baltimore, MD: Johns Hopkins University Press, 2016.

"Litany of St. Joseph." United States Conference of Catholic Bishops. https://www.usccb.org/prayers/litany-saint-joseph.

May, Gerald G. *Addiction and Grace: Love and Spirituality in the Healing of Addictions*. New York: HarperOne, 1988.

May, Gerald G. *Will and Spirit: A Contemplative Psychology*. New York: Harper Collins, 1982.

Macy, Beth. *Dopesick: Dealers, Doctors, and the Drug Company that Addicted America*. New York: Back Bay Books, 2019.

Merton, Thomas. *The Wisdom of the Desert*. New York: New

Directions, 1970.

National Center for Drug Abuse Statistics. "Drug Abuse Statistics." http://drugabusestatistics.org/.

Nouwen, Henri J.M. "The Wounded Healer." Henri Nouwen Society. July 8, 2018. https://henrinouwen.org/meditations/the-wounded-healer/.

Paul VI. *Gaudium et Spes.* Pastoral Constitution. December 7, 1965. vatican.va.

Peterson, Amy. "Golden Scars." Our Daily Bread. October 20, 2020. https://odb.org/US/2020/10/20/golden-scars.

Pia, Faustina Maria. *Jesus, I Trust in You: A 30-Day Personal Retreat with the Litany of Trust.* Steubenville: Emmaus Road Publishing, 2021.

Portier, William L. *Every Catholic an Apostle: A Life of Thomas A. Judge, CM, 1868-1933.* Washington, D.C.: The Catholic University of America Press, 2017.

"Saint Maximilian Mary Kolbe." Franciscan Media. https://www.franciscanmedia.org/saint-of-the-day/saint-maximilian-mary-kolbe.

"Spiritual Awareness/Awakening Quotes." Jesuit Resource. https://www.xavier.edu/jesuitresource/online-resources/quote-archive1/spiritual-awareness-quotes.

Substance Abuse and Mental Health Services Administration. *Key substance use and mental health indicators in the United States: Results from the 2018 National Survey on Drug Use and Health.* Rockville: Center for Behavioral Health Statistics and Quality, Substance Abuse and Mental Health Services Administration, 2019.

Swantek, Fr. Zachary. Conversation with the authors. January 2022.

Tedeschi, Richard G., and Lawrence G. Calhoun. "Posttraumatic Growth: Conceptual Foundations and Empirical Evidence." *Psychological Inquiry* vol. 15, no. 1 (2004): 1–18.

http://www.jstor.org/stable/20447194.

Teresa Benedicta of the Cross (Edith Stein). The Collected Works of Edith Stein, Volume III: The Problem of Empathy. Third revised edition. Trans. Waltraut Stein, Ph.D. Washington, D.C.: ICS Publications, 1989.

Teresa of Calcutta. "Missionaries of Charity." https://www.motherteresa.org/missionaries-of-charity.html.

"The Six Dimensions of Wellness." National Wellness Institute. https://nationalwellness.org/resources/six-dimensions-of-wellness/.

Thérèse of Lisieux. *Story of a Soul*. Huntington, IN: Our Sunday Visitor, 2018.

"Venerable Matt Talbot." Franciscan Media. https://www.franciscanmedia.org/saint-of-the-day/venerable-matt-talbot.

Vogt, Brandon. "St. Lawrence and the True Treasures of the Church." Word on Fire. https://www.wordonfire.org/resources/blog/st-lawrence-and-the-true-treasures-of-the-church/4878/.

von Huben, Ellyn. "9 Things to Know about St. Maximilian Kolbe." Word on Fire. https://www.wordonfire.org/articles/9-things-to-know-about-st-maximilian-kolbe/.

Wakeland, Marcia. "The Art of Listening Deeply with the Vulnerable and Marginalized." *Presence: An International Journal of Spiritual Direction*, June 2017.

Wilson, Bill. *Alcoholics Anonymous Comes of Age: A Brief History of A. A.* New York: Alcoholics Anonymous World Services, 1957.

Yerby, Nathan. "Statistics On Addiction In America." Addiction Center. https://www.addictioncenter.com/addiction/addiction-statistics/.

About the Authors

Keaton Douglas, executive director of the iTHIRST Initiative, a mission of the Missionary Servants of the Most Holy Trinity, is a consultant, educator, counselor, and frequent guest speaker in the field of addiction and recovery, particularly as it pertains to the interface of Catholic spirituality and recovery. She is the creator of the iTHIRST Initiative (The Healing Initiative — Recovery, Spirituality, and Twelve Steps), a comprehensive program which focuses on spirituality in the prevention, treatment, and aftercare of those suffering from substance use disorders and their families.

Keaton holds a Bachelor of Science degree from Georgetown University and a Master of Arts in Theology from the Immaculate Conception Seminary School of Theology at Seton Hall. She is also a CCAR (Connecticut Community Addiction Recovery) Coach.

Keaton has one grown son, Michael, and she and her husband, Tom, live on a small horse farm in Sussex County, New Jersey. To learn more about the iTHIRST Initiative or to contact Keaton, visit iTHIRSTinitiative.org.

***

Lindsay Schlegel is a daughter of God who seeks to encourage, inspire, and lift others up to be all they were created to be through writing, editing, and speaking. She is the author of *Don't Forget to Say Thank You: And Other Parenting Lessons That Brought Me Closer to God* and the host of the podcast *Quote Me with Lindsay Schlegel*. She has written and edited for a variety of print and online publications, including Verily, CatholicMom.com, Aleteia, Vigil, Radiant, Natural Womanhood, Scepter, and

Good & True Media.

Lindsay holds a Bachelor of Arts degree from Boston College. She is currently pursuing a Master of Fine Arts degree with a focus on creative writing from the University of St. Thomas, Houston.

Lindsay lives in New Jersey with her family, and would love to connect at lindsayschlegel.com.